# Ley L

A breakthrough in the literatu
lines, in which the insights of T. C. Lethbridge ...
through a series of pioneering experiments to present new perspectives on the nature and properties of the megalithic ley line system.

# Ley Lines

## their nature and properties

## A Dowser's Investigation

*by*

J. HAVELOCK FIDLER

*Introduction by Paul Devereux*

TURNSTONE PRESS LIMITED
Wellingborough, Northamptonshire

First published 1983
Second Impression 1984

© J. HAVELOCK FIDLER 1983

*This book is sold subject to the condition that it shall not, by way of trade or otherwise, be lent, re-sold, hired out, or otherwise circulated without the publisher's prior consent in any form of binding or cover other than that in which it is published and without a similar condition including this condition being imposed on the subsequent purchaser.*

British Library Cataloguing in Publication Data

Fidler, J. Havelock
  Ley lines
  1. Leys
  930.1      GN776

ISBN 0-85500-173-9

*Turnstone Press is part of the Thorsons Publishing Group*

Printed and bound in Great Britain

# Contents

|  | Page |
|---|---|
| *Acknowledgements* | 9 |
| *Introduction by Paul Devereux* | 11 |

*Chapter*

1. **SLING STONES AND GRAVES** — 17
   *Starting to dowse — Discovering Lethbridge's methods — Use of the long pendulum — Lethbridge's charged sling stones — Discovering charged stones on graves — Charging by handling.*

2. **CONES AND LINES** — 24
   *Underwood's geodetic lines — Use of the Oasis Rod — Geodetic lines in Shieldaig Old Church — Lethbridge's cones — Formation of wedge fields around lines — Overhead lines.*

3. **LEY HUNTING** — 32
   *Watkin's Old Straight Tracks — Ley hunting in Wester Ross — Many lines and ley centres found by dowsing — Sanctuary area round Applecross Abbey — Creating a ley line between charged stones.*

4. **MEASURING THE CHARGE** — 43
   *Radius of gyration of the pendulum as a measure of charge — Statistical techniques — Designing a gyrometer — Variation of psi count with phases of the moon — Development of a reliable technique.*

5. **THE CHARGE IN STONES** — 52
   *Methods of charging and fixing the charge in stones — Charging stones in and around the church — Decay of charge — Festival of Beltane — Work involved in fixing a charge in standing stones — Charging various materials — Lethbridge's interrupters.*

6. **LINES AND THE CHARGE IN STONES**    66
   *The charge on two stones placed together — Concept of power — Two stones separated — Strength of line — External lines — Power of cairns — Loss in strength on separating stones — Effect of adding further stones to line — Measuring strength of a ley line.*

7. **WHAT ARE LEY LINES?**    89
   *The formation of ley lines — Natural or Artificial? — Effect of lining up stones — Strength of stone circle — Problem of lines to old church — Areas of concentrated lines — Blind springs and crossed streams — Wave formation and interference figures — Stonehenge — Supercharging.*

8. **THE PURPOSE OF LEY LINES**    101
   *Various views — Underwood's theories — Tests with mustard seedlings reducing growth.*

9. **INTERRUPTING LEY LINES**    109
   *Masking Lines using quartz chips — Finding the weight of chips needed — Test on a standing stone — explanation of church lines — Easter Island.*

10. **CONCLUSIONS**    120
    *Existence of ley lines confirmed — Must be man-made and man-sited — Lines are energy waves between charged stones — Blind Springs are probably interference figures — Energy possible electromagnetic in form — May be thought-waves — Test on line between two people.*

| | | |
|---|---|---|
| *Appendix A* | MEASURING THE CHARGE | 127 |
| *Appendix B* | LOSS IN STRENGTH OF LINE ON SEPARATING TWO CHARGED STONES | 133 |
| *Glossary* | | 135 |
| *References* | | 141 |
| *Index* | | 143 |

For
ETHEL,
who really started it all.

# Acknowledgements

Apart from Ethel Burton, to whom this work is dedicated, because she really was the basic cause of it all, I must express my thanks to the many friends who have helped by discussing the numerous problems raised during the progress of the work. Amongst these was the late Bernard Smithett, when he was the Secretary of the British Society of Dowsers, and his wife Enid, who gave me the greatest encouragement during their annual visits to this Highland fastness.

Dr Nigel Dower has also discussed and helped with some of the more philosophical aspects of the work. I would also like to thank Mr Hugh C. Maclean, our travelling librarian, for constantly obtaining the most exotic books to aid me in my researches and furthermore for occasionally producing relevant works of which I was quite unaware. Mrs Anne Staveley must also be thanked for struggling with my appalling handwriting and producing a legible typescript, and my wife for ironing out the worst convolutions of my much too academic English.

Finally I must express my enormous indebtedness to the late T. C. Lethbridge, without whose inspiration this work would never have been undertaken, and indeed without whose investigations over the years I would never have become really interested in dowsing.

# Introduction

Dowsing is best known as 'water divining' or 'water witching': the location of underground sources of water by a little-understood sensory process that is better developed in some individuals than in others. In some parts of rural Britain this activity is a normal part of life when drought conditions prevail. The earliest written reference to dowsing in the West is probably in Agricola's *De Re Metallica* (1556), where, in fact, it is described as being used as a means of prospecting for mineral lodes. Today, the Russians use dowsing (or the 'Bio-Physical Method', as they call it) for geological purposes and find it at least as effective as more traditional methods.

But the term 'dowsing' covers a wide spectrum of subtle human sensibilities. We can perhaps accept without too much difficulty that it could be possible for a person standing on a particular site to be able to respond to minute changes in the electromagnetic (EM) environment caused by the presence of moving water or mineral deposits underground. Slight muscular responses are amplified in the motions of various types of dowsing devices — pendulums, spring rods, angle rods and so on — that are in a state of tension or delicate balance. Dowsing, however, is applied to other forms of information-gathering that are perhaps best described as 'divination'. By studying a map or a photograph some dowsers can locate water, oil, lost objects and even murder victims at a distance. I know of one instance where a dowser was able accurately to pinpoint the sunken wreck of a ship on a map at the request of a salvage company that had failed to locate it after a fortnight using sonar and electronic detection systems! This form of remote sensing must employ some type of Extra Sensory Perception that is not necessarily involved in on-site dowsing.

Both types of dowsing undoubtedly work — but not always. They are no more *completely* successful than scientific modes of detection. Moreover, laboratory 'test' conditions do not seem to be conducive to the effective functioning of the dowsing method — we must remember that the human mind is involved, not inanimate pieces of instrumentation. The actuality of the dowsing process, however, can ultimately be evaluated by the fundamental test of whether water, oil or lost objects *are* found where they have been dowsed to be; and, in more cases than coincidence could account for, they are so found.

There is, though, a relatively new area of dowsing in which it is far more difficult to check the effectiveness of the process — 'energy' dowsing. For many years dowsers have been able to find 'noxious rays' emanating from the ground at various places which seem to cause ill-health. Within the last couple of decades or so this branch of the subject has been extended to include the study of megalithic monuments — the standing stone structures dating from prehistoric times that dot the rural landscapes of British and northwestern Europe. A body of information from folklore, physics, anecdotal experience and preliminary scientific investigation, as well as dowsing, suggests that certain of these sites are prone to unusual manifestations of some form of energy. About half a century after their discovery by Alfred Watkins, 'leys' — aligned ancient sites — have also come under the influence of claims and theories to do with 'energies' (Chapter 3). Are leys simply alignments of sites or do they also mark straight lines of force beaming across the countryside from one standing stone monument to the next? Some dowsers — and at the moment the *only* evidence for this idea is dowsing — say 'Yes'.

The trouble with this form of dowsing is that we need to know not only where such phenomena occur, but what the energies *are* that are being detected — a problem not faced in other, more mundane, forms of dowsing. Many dowsers — far too many — are prepared to simply state: 'The energy is here. I know it exists because I have dowsed it.' Such circular attitudes can add nothing more to human knowledge, and if it is left at that we are placed in a mental *cul-de-sac*. We need to know the laws and patterns of behaviour of such dowsed energy, or, if it is an unknown force, whether or not it has side-effects on other, known, energy systems capable of scientific monitoring. It is Dr Fidler's application to these challenges that makes this present book so welcome.

In Chapter 4 Dr Fidler refers to the Dragon Project. This is attempting to look for energies at prehistoric *sites* as opposed to on leys, using dowsing, psychic and scientific monitoring methods. After half a decade the findings of the Project are still extremely tentative; but the Project's co-ordinators have had literally dozens of dowsers, from top-rank professionals to part-time amateurs, study certain stone circles. The co-ordinators are thus almost certainly the most informed people on energy and other types of dowsing at megalithic sites. The hard truth is that dowsers' findings sometimes clash dramatically; yet each practitioner is highly opinionated about what it is they are detecting. In certain respects, dowsers are their own worst enemies. It has become clear to the Dragon Project team that the terminology used in energy dowsing is a shambles and can lead to poor definitions and unnecessary misunderstandings. It needs properly structuring for common usage amongst all energy dowsers so that everyone knows what they are talking about: the American Sig Lonegren (see Chapter 8) is one dowser at least who has made a start on this problem. It has also become clear that if at all possible some form of cross-reference monitoring with other modes of detection are desirable if energy dowsing is to mature into as serious and as usable a bio-sensing tool as, say, water divining. Unfortunately, many dowsers feel this approach is an attempt to 'test' them. This is simply unscientific paranoia — it is not a question of proof but of knowledge, of furthering understanding. Again, it is pleasing to see a dowser of Dr Fidler's calibre making a pioneer effort to see how energies from stone can be studied in ways other than dowsing. Hence his experiments with germination on 'charge lines' emanating from stone, described in Chapter 8, are both convincing and informative.

In addition, Dr Fidler's research put forward in this book has thrown up findings that the Dragon Project, for example, can already begin to relate to. His finding that electromagnetism seems to fix a charge in stone, for instance, may possibly have significance with regard to the Project's confirmation that stone circles are always close to fault lines and thus within the influence of seismo-electricity and other delicate, geologically-originating EM effects. Or, again, Dr Fidler's dowsing measurements of the wavelengths of the charge from stone (Chapter 10), showing results in the radio section of the EM spectrum, might be connected with the Project's discovery of curious ground-level and highly localized radio signals at certain megalithic sites. Dr Fidler seems unsure of such results, though, feeling that if the energy from stones is in the EM spectrum it would surely have been discovered by now. But would it? How could it be if no one makes such measurements at megaliths? Moreover, in the few such monitoring experiments that have been made, various EM anomalies *have* been recorded. The evidence so far does not support Dr Fidler's doubts.

There are theories that leys can be used for telepathic communication and, even more sweepingly, that the lines are 'thought lines', not part of the objective world at all. The first idea simply requires intensive research; the second, if true, presents a fundamental problem. If leys are of the same 'substance' as thought, they *might* simply be mental constructs. Preliminary experimentation by Dr John Steele, one of the Dragon Project's co-ordinators, using biofeedback instrumentation, has indicated that thought forms may be dowsable — he calls them 'virtual objects'. It is thus conceivable that ley dowsers are simply dowsing their own, subconscious, mental artefacts! This would certainly account for the marked disparity of findings from different dowsers working on the same sites that sometimes occurs. I am reassured to some extent, however, in that the method of calibrating his dowsing described by Dr Fidler suppresses the subjective element to a large extent – another instance where this book breaks important new ground.

Dr Fidler comes to some tentative conclusions of his own which one can accept or reject: a dowser's idea of what is being dowsed is not automatically superior to a non-dowser's theory. In the same way, Alfred Watkins' opinion that leys were Neolithic traders' routes need not be accepted. Discovery does not necessarily endow omniscience.

Leys may be merely topographical alignments of sites. Energies may or may not be present at particular sites (it is certainly true that the question of energies along leys and at sites should be treated as separate problems for the time being). But, on the other hand, leys could be making lines of force or charge. It is the presence of this possibility that justifies further research and makes me, personally, welcome a book like this, where the first steps are being taken to explore the wider context in which energy dowsing is being undertaken. I hope Dr Fidler's work will attract the attention of scientists and dowsers alike — for he himself is both. Of one thing I am sure: Dr Fidler's research will fascinate the general reading public. And so it ought, for it deals with remarkable and potentially significant findings.

Paul Devereux<br>
Editor, *The Ley Hunter*<br>
Co-ordinator, *The Dragon Project*

# 1.
# Sling Stones and Graves

Just as I was getting out of the mobile library, Ethel handed me a book, saying, 'Have you read this?' It was a book on dowsing by T. C. Lethbridge. Actually, I had been introduced to the art of dowsing by some friends some twenty years earlier, when I was living in Cardiff, but this had been confined to the use of the 'short' pendulum, i.e. a bob of almost any material on a cord about 8 inches long. These friends were mainly interested in medical diagnosis (radiesthesia), but they pointed out that the pendulum could be used for many other purposes. As a totally inexperienced dowser, I felt that it was inadvisable for me to dabble with my own or other people's health, but I now tried wielding the pendulum over various objects, and soon found that I could in fact dowse. In my hands, however, the pendulum insisted on gyrating in an anti-clockwise direction for the answer 'yes' to my various questions, and oscillate for 'no'. Sometimes the pendulum would gyrate clockwise, but the reason for this I was not to discover until much later, when I had read many of Lethbridge's books.[15] Soon after this I abandoned dowsing, until some twelve or so years later I discovered Lethbridge's books, when I quickly found the subject quite fascinating.

I had recently retired from a long career in agricultural research and was looking round for a suitable subject to occupy my mind in retirement. My wife and I had bought a 100-year-old Presbyterian manse and an abandoned church in the small village of Shieldaig on the north-west coast of Scotland. This church building was to form an essential ingredient in my various researches into dowsing. Lethbridge had also been a retired scientist, and I found that his enquiring mind had investigated many intriguing aspects of dowsing and raised a host of unanswered questions. Here, then was a fascinating field, which I thought I could investigate. Adopting Lethbridge's methods, I soon found that I was a sensitive dowser, but with much to learn about the art.

Lethbridge's methods were different from most other dowsers in that he used what is known as the 'long pendulum'. In this the bob is attached to a cord about 40 inches long. He found that each material over which the bob is held will cause the pendulum to gyrate only if the length of the cord between the hand and the bob is of a specific length, and this he called the 'rate' for the material in question. He went even further than this, maintaining that there are specific rates for male and female and for such abstract concepts as truth, good, evil, death, etc.

It was not long before I had read all Lethbridge's books on dowsing and tried out his concept of rates. I found that these worked perfectly in my hands, but that the pendulum still went 'widdershins' when I had found the right rate for the material under examination. I found that the correct rate could be found by lengthening or shortening the pendulum cord; when it was too short the pendulum oscillated in a vertical direction, i.e. away and towards me; when it was too long, it oscillated at right-angles to this. When the right length had been reached, these two motions combined to make the pendulum gyrate. Later, I discovered that, if the cord was twice as long as the correct rate, the pendulum would gyrate clockwise, and this was also true for a cord half the correct length. These are, of course, harmonic ratios, but whether this is of any significance or not I am not at all sure.

It is generally accepted that all dowsers' 'tools' are no more than magnifiers of his small muscular reactions to signals from the subconscious. Whether the 'harmonic' reactions are simply a reflection of a somewhat mathematical subconscious mind, I would not hazard a guess, but I found that these reactions worked well with me and enabled me to find many more rates than those published by Lethbridge.

One point I should make clear before going further is that I am in the habit of measuring my rates, i.e. the length of the cord, in centimetres. This was greatly disapproved of by Lethbridge and he spent several pages of one of his books saying just what he thought of the metric system in general. His main point was that the range of rates was between 0 and 40 inches and that, if these are marked out on a circle divided into 40 points, contrasting concepts occur at opposite sides of the circle: e.g. life at 20, and death at 40. He maintained that this relationship would not work out if a centimetre scale were used. As a scientist I have always used the metric scale and found this very convenient for measuring the length of the pendulum cord. Forty inches, as used by Lethbridge, is virtually the same as 100 centimetres (39.3708 inches), so there is little over half an inch difference in the longest rate, particularly as I measure my cord to the centre of gravity of the bob. Moreover, the ratio of opposite concepts works just as well: i.e. life is at 50 and death at 100 centimetres.

The harmonic ratios, I often find, are very useful in the field. A long cord of, say, 100cm is very difficult to control in a wind, unless one has a very heavy bob at the end of it. I usually use a bob weighing about 50g (2oz), and this gets blown about, so that it is difficult to interpret its movement. If, however, the cord is shortened by a half, a positive reaction is given if it gyrates in a clockwise direction. One can even go down to a quarter-length cord, when the gyration will again be anti-clockwise.

In one of his books Lethbridge describes how he and his wife found what he thought must be sling stones outside a hill fort some distance from the sea. These were rounded pebbles, obviously taken from the sea beaches, and he considered that they must have been brought up to the fort by men to use in its defence. He tested these stones with his pendulum and found that they gave a reaction to the male rate (60cm) and in addition a reaction to that for anger. Smaller stones gave only the male reaction, and he suggested that these had been used by boys practising their sling throwing. He and his wife confirmed this 'charging' of stones by each throwing at a wall stones collected (and previously untouched) from the sea shore. In each case a male or female reaction was given by the stone when tested with the pendulum. My wife and I repeated Lethbridge's experiment of throwing previously untouched stones collected from the sea shore and found that they gave the appropriate reaction with the pendulum. In addition, I happened to have a flint arrowhead, collected when I was living in South Wales. I tested this with my pendulum, using a cord 60 cm long, and found a strong male reaction. This meant that the original imprint had persisted in this stone for some three or four thousand years.

About this time I had become interested in certain heaps of stones, which I had noticed scattered round some parts of the countryside near to Shieldaig. These heaps of stones appeared to be of two different kinds, the first of which was at the sides of cultivated ground, the heaps being of all sizes, as were the stones of which they were composed. These stones had obviously been mixed with the fine soil when the ice retreated at the end of the last Ice Age, picked out by the crofters as the ground was laboriously cultivated, and piled at the sides of the fields.

The other heaps were rather different from these piles of clearance stones. The stones here were more or less uniform in size, usually about 2 to 4 inches across, and the heaps about 6 to 8 feet long and about 3 to 4 feet wide; very noticeably, the long dimension ran approximately east and west. Testing these heaps with my pendulum gave a reaction for death (rate of 100 cm). I came to the conclusion, therefore, that these heaps had been used for burial, in the absence of any recognized and easily available burial ground in the immediate district, Applecross being some sixteen miles away over the hills.

To explain this means going into the intricacies of local history. The area round Applecross was greatly influenced by the foundation of an abbey by St Maelrubha, one of the early Irish saints. This foundation persisted until the Reformation and the death of the last abbot in 1567. After this date there appears to have been no ecclesiastical representation in the Shieldaig area until the government built a Telford church and manse in the village in 1823. During the intervening period, Christianity appears, as far as one can judge, to have been rather in abeyance, and some of the old pagan beliefs were revived, in addition to an increase in witchcraft, which was never very far below the surface in the Western Highlands. Burial in consecrated ground would not therefore have been considered important or necessary.

I had also become interested in the technique of dating with the pendulum and had worked out a method for such estimations based on the binary system.[8] On applying this technique to some sixty or so of these graves, I obtained dates falling between 1600 and 1800.

My pendulum had also indicated a male rate on all of the stones from these dated graves, as well as a female rate on about half of them. In no case did I find a female rate alone. I came to the conclusion that this imprint of both male and female on about half of these heaps of stones was possibly due to the Highland custom of men burying the women, whereas there was no case of a female-only stone heap, i.e. of women burying women. Here, then, was a good example of stones having absorbed a sex imprint of both the body buried in the grave and also of the man who had carried out the burial. I was later to confirm this supposition by testing the stones on modern graves, where the sex of the internant is identifiable from the gravestone. The stones on these graves I had been examining were apparently imprinted in the same way as with the sex of the thrower of Lethbridge's sling stones, and I decided, therefore, to investigate the imprint in more detail.

I soon found that it was not necessary to throw the stone at a wall to imprint it. If the stone was held in the hand and hit smartly with a hammer, a good imprint was obtained. If, however, a previously unhandled stone was placed on the ground and hit, even with a seven-pound sledge hammer, no imprint was obtained. This observation soon led me to discover that one could imprint an untouched stone by hammering it on the ground alongside another stone previously imprinted by my wife with the female rate, the uncharged stone received a female imprint, although it was I who had done the hammering. On the other hand, if I handled the stone first and then placed it alongside a female-imprinted stone and then hammered it, the stone would take both a male and a female imprint, the pendulum gyrating with the cord lengths of both 60 and 72.5cm. This produced stones similar in imprint to those found on graves where a woman had presumably been buried.

Lethbridge found that all living material has an inherent male or female rate and that this is maintained even after death. As an agricultural scientist I was well aware that all soil is made up of ground-down rocks and the decayed remains (humus) of plant material and the micro-organisms that live in the soil. If all these maintained in their dead bodies their inherent sex rate, all soil would become charged with both the male and female rates. That this is not the case can be readily discovered by holding a pendulum of the correct length over some soil. What, therefore, happens to the dead material in the soil? As everyone knows, it gradually breaks down to simple chemicals to form humus. In doing so does this material loose its inherent sex rate?

To test this, I first examined a sample of freshly-cut grass mowings and found that this gave a strong reaction with the pendulum at both the male and female rates. This was hardly surprising considering the number of weeds in my lawn. I then examined a well-rotted sample from the base of our compost heap, which is made mainly from just such lawn mowings. There was only the faintest reaction to either of the sex rates, and a sod from our peat stack gave no reaction at all, as was also the case with a lump of coal. This seemed to indicate that as the dead material breaks down into simpler chemicals, the sex reaction is gradually lost.

This conclusion is illustrated by a quite simple experiment. Take an ordinary wooden match and test its sex rate with the pendulum. In the one I tried, the wood (spruce?) gave a female reaction. Now strike the match and allow it to burn out completely. This can be done by holding in a pair of pliers and changing ends when the match is half burnt. Do not place the match on anything while it is burning (for example, a plate), because this would then become fixed with the charge, as I will show later. When cold, remove the burnt-out head, which might complicate matters, and again test the stick of the match for sex reaction. It now consists of almost pure carbon, perhaps with a few other trace elements, and it will be found that there is now no sign of the original sex reaction.

As my wife pointed out, this would seem to dispose of my theory devised to account for the sex reaction found in stones from the so-called graves, described above. I do not, however, think this is so. The bones of an interred body usually last a considerable time and in a peaty soil, such as is almost universal in our locality, whole bodies have been found, complete with clothing after thousands of years of burial. The graves I described can all be classed as archaeologically very recent and it would seem almost certain that some remains of the body would still be present in sufficient quantity to give the sex reaction. This could, of course, only be proved by detailed excavation of the site.

In most of his books Lethbridge points out that there is a circular field round an object, the radius of which is equal to the rate. Anywhere inside this circle the pendulum will gyrate if the cord is of the appropriate length, while outside this circle no reaction is obtained. I discovered that if a stone is hammered just outside this circle, no imprint is obtained, whereas the stone can be placed anywhere within the circle and it takes on the imprint of the 'parent' stone. It was the problem of these circular fields and their inter-relationships that I had to investigate next.

## 2.
# Cones and Lines

Another book to which Ethel introduced me, was one by the late Guy Underwood.[26] This dowser had spent many years investigating the geodetic lines he found below such prehistoric sites as stone circles, including Stonehenge, barrows, dolmen, menhirs, etc., as well as pre-Reformation churches. He noticed three distinct types of geodetic line: (1) water lines (2) track lines and (3) aquastats. The first of these, he considered, were the normal underground streams encountered by water diviners, while the second were tracks which were often followed by animals and which sometimes developed into those frequented by man. Aquastats, in spite of their name, do not appear to be connected with underground water, and it does not seem clear why Underwood chose this name for them.

Each geodetic line is made up of a number of 'parallels', and each of these is triple in form, being called a triad by Underwood. Water lines are made up of three lines, each one being a triad (Figure 1), while track lines have only two such parallel lines of triads. Aquastats have four lines, each again being a triad. Underwood was at pains to point out that these geodetic lines, although travelling in a specific direction, do not proceed directly but wind and zig-zag, often in a very complex way. Water lines, he considered, were 'positive' and mainly affected the left hand of the dowser, whereas track lines and aquastats were negative and affected the right hand.

(a) WATER LINE  (b) TRACK LINE

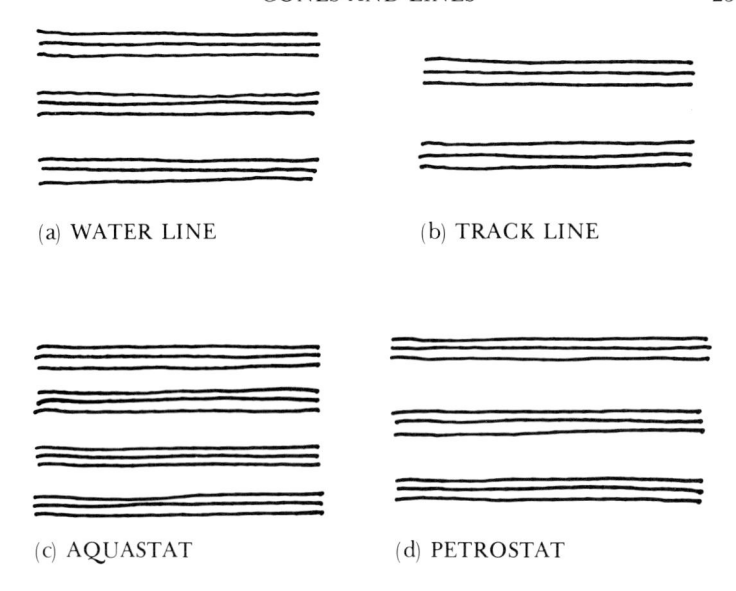

(c) AQUASTAT  (d) PETROSTAT

Figure 1. Construction of geodetic lines.

Underwood went on to describe many different forms of convolutions in the main courses of his geodetic lines. Amongst these the most important is what he called a 'blind spring', this being a centre on which primary lines converge. This was, he thought, in the form of a spiral with numerous coils. He goes on to state that the blind spring was an esoteric centre of the Old Religion, forming the most important part of an ancient monument, this becoming 'holy ground'.

Underwood also described a number of instruments which he used in his work and which he found much more sensitive than the normal hazel or willow twigs used by water diviners. Amongst these he described the 'Oasis Rod', which I found so interesting that I soon made myself one (Figure 2). Full details of its construction are given in my article in the *Journal of the British Society of Dowsers*,[9] but briefly it consists of a springy strip of brass attached at one end to an axle that can freely rotate within a wooden handle, this being held in one hand in a horizontal position. To the other end of the brass spring is attached a light cord about 8 inches long, the end of which is held between the finger and thumb of the other hand. In use,

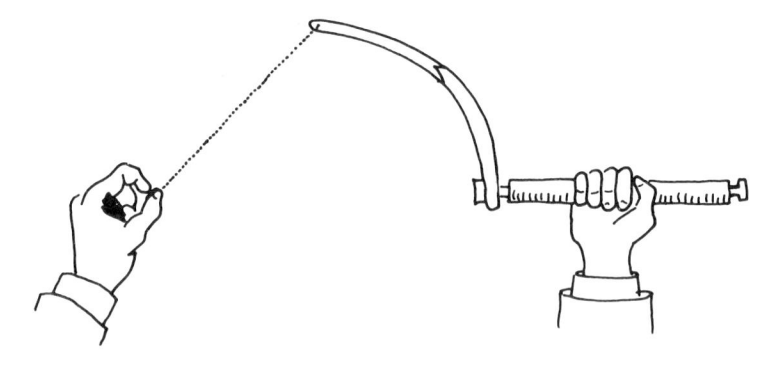

Figure 2. Underwood's Oasis Rod.

the held end of the cord must be exactly in line with the axle, with enough tension to keep the spring in the form of a quarter circle. If the cord hand is not in line, the spring will flap about quite uncontrollably. The art, which is learnt after a little practice, is to keep the spring in a horizontal position, when minute alterations in the muscle tension of the arm will cause it to rise or fall. It would appear from Underwood's illustrations that he kept the spring pointing inwards towards the body, whereas I prefer to have it pointing outwards. After some years of use with the Oasis Rod, I have found this instrument extremely sensitive. As soon as it reaches a line, it flips down and can readily pick up the three lines of a triad which are only a few inches apart.

Underwood's main thesis was that the layout of all ancient sites were designed to coincide with the underlying geodetic lines. As mentioned above, part of my Highland property is a disused church building. Having mastered the use of the Oasis Rod, I thought I would see what, if any, geodetic lines I could find in it. As the church was built only about a hundred years ago, when presumably the masons and architects were no longer familiar with the ancient lore, this church would probably not knowingly be placed on what the ancients would have considered to have been a suitable site. It need hardly be said that I found no sign of geodetic lines as described by Underwood, but what I did find was to set me off on the main lines of my future researches.

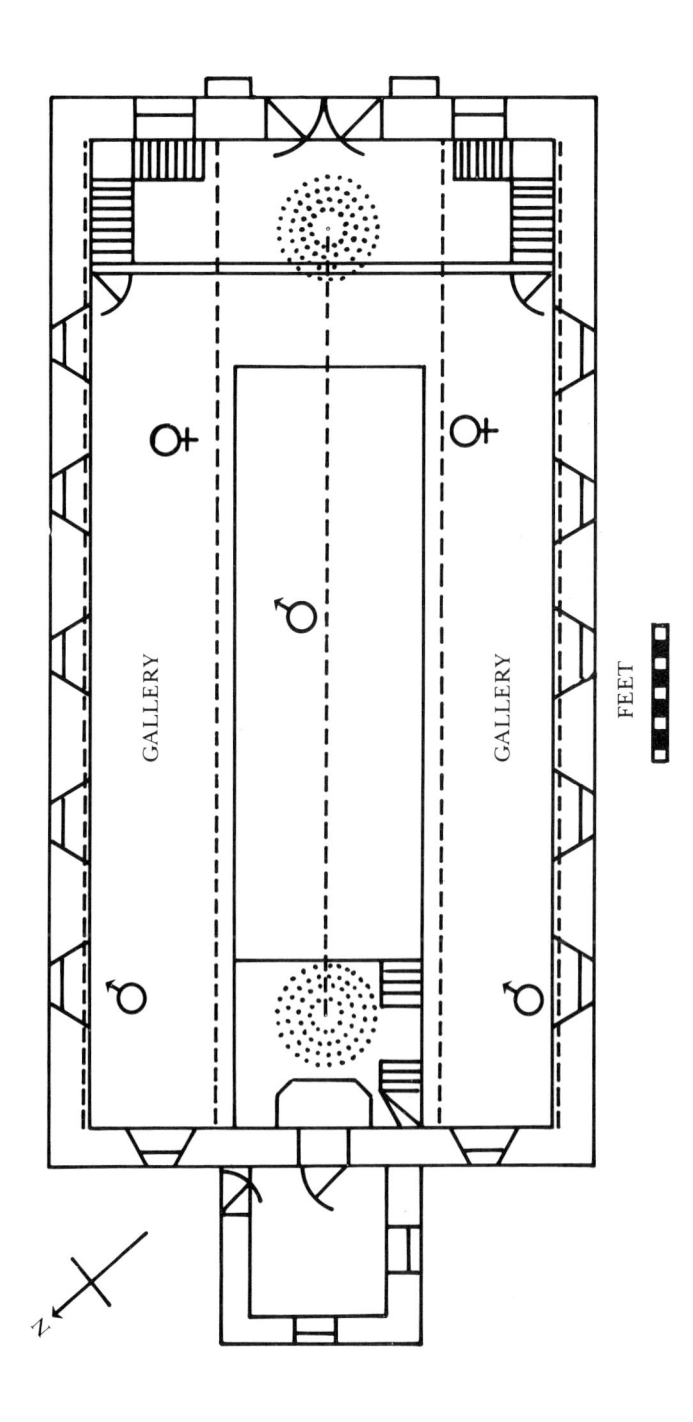

Figure 3. Plan of Shieldaig Old Church, showing geodetic lines and blind springs.

Before detailing these discoveries it would be appropriate to describe this church building, since it was to form such an important part of my future work. It consists of a massive — the walls are over 3 feet thick — rectangular building about 75 x 40 feet with the long axis roughly north-west to south-east. There is a small vestry on the north-west end (Figure 3). It is constructed of rectangular, dressed Torridonian Sandstone blocks as facings, with rough stones mortared together inside. Torridonian Sandstone is one of the oldest rocks in the British Isles and forms most of the mountains in the area. It is extremely hard. The other local rock is Lewisian Gneiss, which forms the bedrock on which the church lies. This latter rock is even more ancient, being formed in the Pre-Cambrian era, and is greatly contorted, thus being unsuitable for building purposes.

Inside the front door of the church is a vestibule with stairs leading up on either side to a tiered gallery some 9½ feet from floor level. This gallery runs round three sides of the building and is supported on cast-iron pillars. There was originally a partition wall cutting off the vestibule from the main church area, with a door on either side, but this was removed at some date after the building ceased to be used as a church, to allow access for cars, the building now being used as a garage. At the north-west end is a raised area which was probably reserved for the Elders of the Church, and in the centre of this is a smaller raised platform with immediate access to the vestry door.

To return to my discoveries with the Oasis Rod, I found that there was a line down the centre of the building that reacted to the male rate of the pendulum and that there were two similar lines down the side walls. Immediately below the outer edge of the gallery and running between the iron pillars was a line which reacted to the female rate on the pendulum. Further, at each end of the central line was a blind spring in the form outlined by Underwood. One of these had its centre in the middle of the vestibule and the other just on the edge of the raised platform outside the vestry. Each of these lines was a triad with side lines (parallels) a foot or more on either side. I could find no sign of any lines in the vestry.

The question immediately arose as to the nature of these

lines. Were they geodetic lines running through the underlying rock, or did they run somewhere through the air within the building? They certainly did not fit in with the main characteristics of the three types of geodetic lines described by Underwood, in that there was a central triad with parallel triads on either side at a distance of about a foot. These lines to some extent resembled Underwood's water lines, but I could not detect any sign of underground water below the church, even under the blind springs. If these lines were not geodetic in nature, were they some form of aerial line?

After much thought on this problem, I recalled a diagram reproduced in several of Lethbridge's books. He had discovered that the circular field surrounding an object such as a charged stone is really the base of a cone that extends vertically upwards above the object. There is also a similar, but inverted, cone extending below the object. The radius of the base of the cone is just equal to the rate, i.e. it is 60cm for a

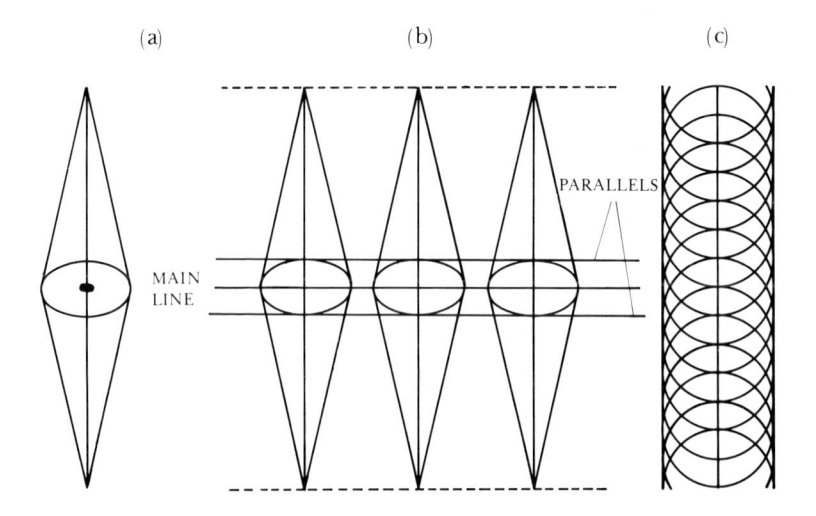

Figure 4.(a) Lethbridge's cones.
   (b) Development of wedge from cones on a line.
   (c) Formation of parallels from cone bases on a line.

male imprinted stone and 72.5cm for a female (Figure 4a). Lethbridge did not, as far as I am aware, estimate the height of these cones, but, by placing a stone on the floor of the church below the gallery, I was able to measure the radius of the cone above and to calculate by means of a little simple trigonometry that the tip of the cone surrounding the male stone was about 13½ metres above. By placing the stone on the gallery and measuring the radius of the cone below it, I was able to confirm that the lower cone was similar in size to that above. I also repeated this exercise with a female-imprinted stone and was surprised to find that the tip of the cone was approximately at the same height as that of the male stone in spite of the fact that the base of the female cone is larger (radius of 72.5cm).

Underwood, in describing how the parallels of a water line are formed, published a figure which looks like a number of overlapping circles (Figure 4c). If these are interpreted as the bases of a number of overlapping cones, it is possible to suggest that a line is really an infinite number of overlapping cones lying side by side along the line which joins the centre of their bases. Thus, the field surrounding a line would then be in the form of a wedge rising above its base, with a similar wedge below (Figure 4b). The parallels would then be the outsides of the bases of the individual cones and should, therefore, be at a distance equal to the rate.

Now, on measuring the distances of the parallels of the central male line on the gallery above, I was surprised to find that these were larger than the widths at floor level and, moreover, that the angle of increase was approximately the same as that for the cone below the male stone previously measured. The conclusion was that I was here dealing with an inverted wedge and that the actual line was situated in the air above gallery level. I then made the assumption that the distance of the parallels from the central line **at the level of the line** was that of the rate, i.e. 60cm with the male and 72.5cm with the female line. If this was the case, the lines would appear to run just above the level of the eaves of the building. When I later found other lines at ground level, I was able to confirm that the distance of the parallels from the central triad was in fact the same as the appropriate rate.

These lines I had found in my stone-built church differed

from all three of the geodetic lines described by Underwood. They seemed to be closely connected with the cones found above and below the imprinted stones, and I formed the theory that they were the summation of all the forces of the stones making up the structure of the church. These stones must have received many blows with hammer and chisel when they were cut by the masons a hundred years ago, and during this process, become imprinted with the male rate in the same way as I had imprinted 'sling' stones. The female lines under the gallery were possibly a balancing force neutralizing the whole. I therefore decided to call these lines 'petrostats', to differentiate them from the three types of geodetic lines described by Underwood.

The explanation of lines as a series of closely overlapping cones does not, however, account for the phenomenon of blind springs. These appear to be about 1½ metres in radius and always seem to occur at the terminus of a line. Although, as will be seen in the next chapter, blind springs form an essential ingredient of ley lines, I have not as yet been able to do any detailed work on this subject. My feeling is that they are some form of 'field' phenomenon which differs from the cone base round a charged object, and only develops when the line terminates.

Much of the work outlined in this chapter was described in a talk I gave to the British Society of Dowsers at their Spring Congress in Stirling in 1975. After the talk one of the members asked in what way these lines I had described differed from ley lines. At that time I knew very little about ley lines, and I also thought that I was dealing with some form of aquastat. I therefore replied that, although my lines run straight, aquastats according to Underwood usually go in curves or zig-zags. I was probably right in my statement, but I had not really answered his question. When I got home, I thought I had better find out something about ley lines.

# 3.
# Ley Hunting

As usual, Ethel produced the relevant literature. This proved to be Alfred Watkin's *The Old Straight Track*.[21] Watkins was, besides being an expert photographer, a miller's representative, who spent much of his time travelling the countryside around Hereford in the early years of this century. He was much interested in the various antiquities he encountered on his travels, and one day, when looking out over the rolling country before him, he was inspired by the thought that many of these antiquities were sited on straight lines, to which he gave the name 'leys', running across the countryside. Later, when he checked this on the map, he found the idea appeared to be true. Much of the rest of his life was spent in following up this theory.

The antiquities he found which conformed to this pattern were prehistoric mounds, camp sites, pre-Reformation churches, castles, wayside crosses, old wells, fords, and some old tracks. In certain cases groups of trees seemed to be on these lines, and of great importance were standing stones and stone circles. Admittedly, not all these features could be considered to be of similar antiquity, but he pointed out, for instance, that many early churches had been built on sites of much greater age.

His interest spread locally, and the Straight Track Club was formed, the members following up many of these lines in the field. By the time of the Second World War interest had declined, but in the late 1960s and 1970s had revived again, and now there are many workers engaged in the mapping of these lines and similar phenomena. A number of magazines and journals, such as *The Ley Hunter,* publish the results of this work.

The classical method of detecting a ley line is to examine a map of the area, usually the 1:50,000, and to mark on this any of the features listed above that have been recorded by the Ordnance Survey. Then, starting with a promising site, one looks to see what other marked features are in alignment with it. Generally, five such features within a distance of 25 miles are required before a 'ley line' can be suspected. Field investigation is then necessary with very accurate compass work. This is of particular importance, since even on a large-scale map the thinnest pencil line represents an area many metres wide, and a map symbol such as a church covers a much greater area on the map than does the actual building. Further, it is not unknown for the position of a feature shown on the O.S. map to be misleading (for example, standing stones could have been moved from their original position). There are many difficulties and uncertainties to be overcome, and Watkins outlined some of these in his book *The Ley Hunter's Manual.*[25]

For the next two years I became an enthusiastic ley hunter. I soon discovered that I could not use the classical methods described above because, on examining the O.S. map of the district, I could find virtually none of the necessary features listed by Watkins. The sole exceptions were a few cairns that might, or might not, be of ancient origin. I had, however, on my walks found two obvious, but unrecorded, standing stones, one at Arina on the North Applecross coast, and, most conveniently, a small one of classic form on the hillside about 100 metres above my house. As neither of these was visible from the other, I had to devise my own techniques. This is where my dowsing experience became useful.

To start with I walked round the stone above my house, holding the Oasis Rod, and noted the exact points at which this dipped. Using a theodolite placed over the centre of the standing stone, the angles between true north and these suspected ley lines were carefully noted. In fact, seven such lines were noted radiating from this stone, three pairs being opposite each other; in other words, three lines passed straight through the stone and one stopped at it. I later found, however, by very careful dowsing, that the line running almost north and south, was, in fact, a triple line, there being only just over 3° between each of the three lines.

The next task was to find out where these lines went to. One was fairly obvious; to the north-west is a gap in the hills on the horizon, and through this gap can be seen the crest of a small conical hill, which proved to be Meall Mor (Big Hill) at Fearnmore. I soon set off down the new coast road leading to Applecross, and checked with my Oasis Rod that a line did in fact pass over the top of this hill at the correct angle. There was no standing stone or cairn on the top of this hill, which was formed of flat rock, but I came to the conclusion that it was a perfect site for a beacon, which would be visible over a wide area in most directions. I later discovered that, standing by my home stone, which I called Rhu-na-Bidh (Point of Pitch) Stone, the sun was seen to set exactly over Meall Mor on 1 May. I am not a sufficiently competent astronomer to know whether this would have been the case in megalithic days, but there was a strong suggestion here that this line was connected with the ancient festival of Beltane, when beacons were lit and various festive rituals were carried out. The line there appears to carry on out over the Sound of Raasay to reach the north end of the island of Rona, near where the present lighthouse is situated, but I have not been able to check it there on the ground as yet, since this is not an area of very easy access.

Tracing this line back towards the south-east, I found that it appeared to run towards a notch (another of Watkins' features) on the eastern side of Ben Shieldaig, but, when I climbed up to this notch, I could find no line present. I had, however, discovered that I could detect a line even when I was some distance from it, by using a well-known dowsing technique. A short pendulum is held in the right hand and the left arm extended; then, as one turns through a complete circle, the pendulum gyrates only when the left hand is pointing towards the line, or object, sought. Standing in the empty notch, I did this, and found that the line was more to the east. I moved about ten metres south and got a cross-bearing, which indicated that the ley centre was on the top of a small hill just to my east. Climbing this, I found that it was crowned with three boulders, each about two metres across. This was the ley centre, and using my Oasis Rod I soon found my line, as well as others radiating from here.

The next lines to be checked were the closely adjoining three running more or less north and south and crossing at the Rhu-na-Bidh Stone (Figure 5). I had already noted a square stone lying on the top of a small headland about half-way down the Aird peninsula, just beyond Camus Beithe (Bay of the Birches). The most westerly of my lines appeared to run in this direction, and I soon confirmed with my Oasis Rod that this was the case. However, I found that the centre from which the lines radiated was not in the stone, but some 10 centimetres from its side. Close inspection showed that the stone

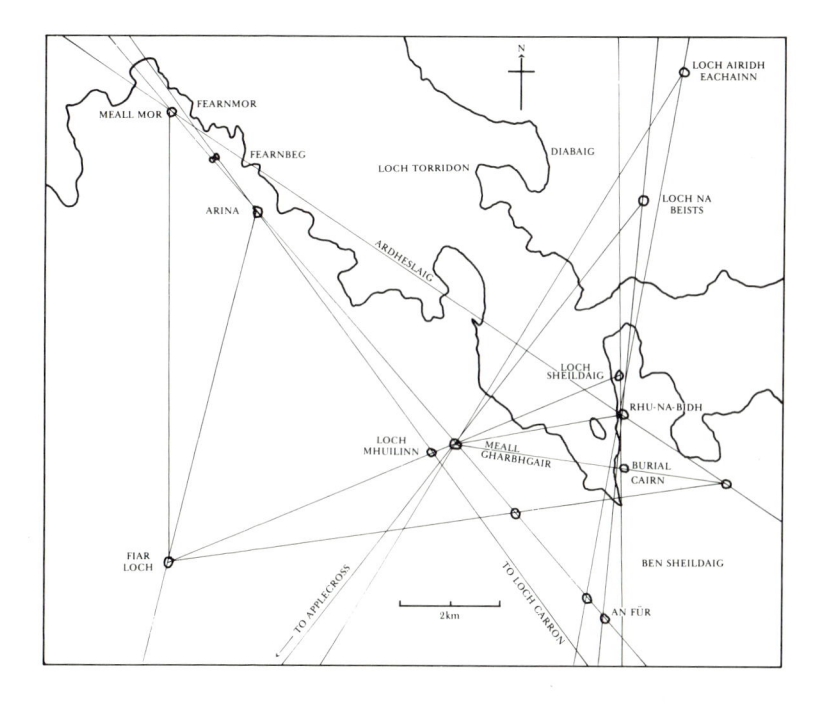

Figure 5. Principal ley lines found in North Applecross.

was lying on top of the peat, which suggested that it had in fact been displaced from its original position, since the peat is generally considered to have been formed after the Bronze Age.

This line goes on to cross the narrows between Loch Shieldaig and Loch Torridon and continues on the Diabaig side, where I again found it. The central of the three lines from Rhu-na-Bidh first runs over a small hill, Cnoc Ruadh (Red Stone), where my wife found a standing stone of classic shape, but recumbant, and then over to the Diabaig side of the loch. Here it crosses a number of other lines, each crossing being marked with a large stone, and then reaches a stone at the side of Loch-na-Beiste (Loch of the Beast). Jenkins[15] noted, when ley hunting in Argyle, that lines are often to be found in connection with features named in the Gaelic after the Beast, the Horse and the Old Woman. My Loch-na-Beiste is a small deep lochan below a steep cliff and could be just the place to contain a water kelpie.

The most easterly of the three lines goes on the Diabaig side to Loch Airdh nan Eachan (the Loch of the Field of the Little Horse, again one of Jenkins' features). This stone was of some interest, since it was in the shape of a dolmen, a flat stone about 2½ metres across, perched on top of two smaller stones. I have not yet been able to find a feature on the map named after the Old Woman (Cailleach), which Jenkins considered to be of great importance since it was connected with the Old Religion and the White Goddess. 'Cailleach' is also the Gaelic name given to the corn dollies at harvest time. Incidentally, this line running to Loch Airdh nan Eachan passes through a cairn on Sidean Mor (Hill of the Fairies).

I should here confess that I do not speak the Gaelic, which I find a most difficult language, owing to the phonetic spelling and involved grammar. However, by browsing through Dwelly's *Dictionary*, which is really a Gaelic encyclopaedia, one can usually deduce the probable meaning of a name. The Gaelic names, as with other Celtic languages, are usually descriptive, and, if one can translate them, interesting information about the site is often discovered.

I also traced these three lines to the south, again finding features of interest. The most easterly, i.e. the one continuing through Rhu-na-Bidh from the Camus Beithe Stone, goes on through the village to an early Bronze Age ring cairn. I had already noted this and reported it, since there was danger of its destruction to make room for new council houses. An official rescue excavation was carried out by archaeologists in the autumn of 1978 and the area subsequently preserved. This line then crosses the loch to a point where a neolithic flint knapping factory has been found, over an old well, and then up a valley in the hills to a large square stone, where it crosses another line, which I shall mention later.

The other two lines also cross the loch, and I picked them up again on the ridge at about 380 metres above the sea. The central line enters an area marked on the map as An Für, and here I found a most impressive stone perched on the very edge of the ridge overlooking the lochs. An Für, according to Dwelly's dictionary, means 'welcome' or 'hospitality'. This seemed a most unlikely meaning for a rather bleak and inhospitable area of mountainside, and I wondered if perhaps the surveyor had mistaken this word for An Faire, which means the 'look-out' or 'guard point'. This at first seemed a likely meaning, since from this point one gets a superb view of the Outer Loch Torridon, with Skye and the Outer Hebrides beyond. There are also some remains of the site of an ancient fort in this area. A still better view is, however, obtained about a kilometre to the west, where there is a cairn, through which my third line passes. If anywhere, this should have been entitled An Faire, and I decided to refer this name to this cairn in future.

However, I subsequently discovered that the name An Für for this site was not so incongruous as I had at first thought. A friend lent me a rather poor typescript (since lost) of a history of Applecross, and in this it was mentioned that there was an area of sanctuary within a radius of six miles round the ancient abbey. I measured out this radius on the map, taking for the centre the present burial ground and cross, but it did not seem to pass through any features of interest. However, I later discovered that the Old Scottish Mile was 1984 yards, and if I used six of these miles as my radius, it just passed through the An Für Stone. If this stone was, in fact, marking the boundary of the sanctuary area it could well be described as 'hospitable'.

I later discovered some five other ley centres on the northern half of the circle, with lines running like the spokes of a wheel, with Applecross as the hub. The southern part is much less accessible, but I found three standing stones in a line east of Toscaig marking the boundary of this circle. The lines between stones are, of course, straight, although together they make up a circle six miles in radius. Six Old Scots miles work out at just about 13,130 megalithic yards.[25] John Michell,[17] however, points out that one geomancer's mile equals 5,280 megalithic yards, so six Scots miles is very nearly equal to 2½ geomancer's miles or 5,280 megalithic rods. This sanctuary area may, therefore, have a very ancient origin.

Just south of the An Für Stone the line crosses a small loch, called Lochan Prapa on the O.S. map. As far as I can discover, there is no such word as Prapa in the Gaelic, but Dwelly gives Prabha as meaning 'the little people', perhaps a not insignificant meaning in this context. I wondered, therefore, if this is perhaps another case of the surveyor having written down the sound of the word given him, without understanding the meaning.

One of the first standing stones I investigated was just north of the new road to Applecross at Arina. This is a very well marked stone about 1½ metres high, standing on the top of a small rounded hill. Amongst the lines I found radiating from this stone were two with only 3° between them, running 139° and 142° east of north respectively. There was also one running off in the direction of Applecross. During my later excursions I was able to follow up both of these closely adjoining lines, and I found them to be of great interest. To the north-west the 142° line passes through the little township of Fearnmore, where there is a fine standing stone sited between the houses. It then carries on out to sea. There is no land here for nearly 40 miles, but on extending the line, it crosses the east coast of the Outer Hebridean island of Lewis and then to the great megalithic complex at Callanish. I have not so far been able to visit that area to check whether this line is in fact detectable there.

Following these two lines to the south-east, they pass through a pair of small, and rather dilapidated, cairns on hillocks south-west of Fearnbeg. The 139° line passes over a small mountain by the name of Meall Gharbhgair (Hill of the Rough Ground), which looks as if it may have been another beacon hill, and which is the meeting point of several more lines. It then passes through the cairn mentioned above, to which I had given the name An Faire, and also the stone at An Für. The 142° line passes just south of Meall Gharbhgair, where there is a fine cairn near the edge of Loch a' Mhuilinn (Loch of the Mill). How old this cairn is I do not know, but it is in excellent repair, and I noted that the lichens growing on it have spread from one stone to the next, covering the gaps. Lichens are very slow in growth, often adding only a few inches to their size in a hundred years; so this cairn may be of considerable age. This 142° line goes on to pass south of An Für, and, where it crosses the three line from the Rhu-na-Bidh Stone, I located small crossing stones. I was able to pick it up again just south of the road to Lochcarron; here on the side of the limestone ridge I discovered a small burial cairn and a spring with a stone wall beside it. The line ran through both and continued in the direction of Lochcarron, where it passes over the Ploc (a small peninsula), and on the other side of the loch, up into the remote mountains south of Attadale. I had thus traced this line for over 17 miles and identified some ten ley features on it.

Such Plocs seem to be favoured by the megalithic linesmen, since I discovered a line running over the one at Fasag at the eastern end of Loch Torridon. This line crosses the loch to Annat (Mother Church), but does not, as might be expected, go to the site of the old chapel at the western end of the burial ground. Instead it goes to a large flat stone about 2 metres in diameter at the eastern end of the burial ground. According to all the dowsers to whom I have shown this stone, it is not a burial site, but has a strong sacred influence, although one dowser said she found it very evil. Whatever its origin, this stone marks a ley centre where a number of lines cross.

Many dowsers who have investigated ley lines, state that at each ley centre there are crossed water lines and that each centre is surrounded by a spiral of lines similar to what Underwood called a blind spring. I also have checked this at quite a number of sites and in every case have confirmed this finding. However, I did discover that there were many minor sites where only two lines cross, where in every case except one I have found the point marked by a stone, but in all these there was no sign of crossed water lines or a blind spring. Tom Graves[12] has suggested that ley centres are in fact areas where there is some form of underground energy and that standing stones were used by their megalithic builders to tap this energy and bring it to the surface, where it then travelled in straight lines from one stone to the next as 'overgrounds' and was detectable by the dowser as a ley line.

Most modern writers have dismissed Watkins' theory that ley lines were ancient tracks used by travellers of various kinds. This can hardly be the full explanation, since, as I have shown above, in this particular area they frequently travel over the sea. However, I do not think he was entirely wrong. As I have described, ley lines can be detected by a dowser even when he is not actually standing on the line, and also it is generally thought that the art of dowsing was much more common in ancient times than is now the case. Since there were, of course, no signposts or maps in those days, a knowledge of the local lines could have been used rather like an A.A. itinerary: thus, starting at a given stone etc., the traveller would know that he had to move along a certain line until he reached some other feature; he would then move along another line, and so on until he reached his destination. This method would have the great advantage in that the 'track' could be followed in the dark or in a thick mist.

I spent much time during this period investigating the behaviour of the lines flowing from the stone behind my house. Amongst other things I found that these lines reacted to either the male or the female rate and usually changed from one to the other when they passed through the stone. Moreover, they were formed of triads, with further parallel triads some 60 or 72.5cm on either side for the male or female lines respectively, just as I had found with the petrostats I had investigated inside the church building. Also, these parallel lines became closer to the central line when the ground was above or below the level of the stones they originated from. I was able to use this observation to discover whether ley lines travel at a uniform height over the intervening ground or travel direct from one stone to the next, irrespective of the irregularities of this ground. I found two adjoining lines, one of which went to the burial cairn in the village almost at sea level, and another which went to An Für at an altitude of 380 metres. Using the same techniques as that which I had used in the church to find the height of the petrostats there, I found that the ley lines did in fact travel directly through the air from one centre to the next, irrespective of the contours of the intervening countryside.[10]

The methods I had been using, i.e. plotting all the lines round each ley centre I found, produced a considerable number of such lines. The theoretical average of seven lines per centre meant that their total increased by seven each time a new centre was found. In practice it was not quite as bad as this, the method being subject to the law of diminishing returns, since more and more of these lines were found to run to centres I had already located. In certain areas, particularly those that had obviously been well inhabited in the past (as shown by the number of ruined crofts), the lines were very numerous, and I had to use the 1:10,000 map to plot them. After two seasons of such ley hunting I came to the conclusion that, to paraphrase the well-known quotation from the book of Ecclesiastes: 'Of hunting of many ley lines there is no end; and much measuring is a weariness of the flesh', and I did not see that I was getting any further in my studies of this phenomenon by such work.

One day when I was out for a walk with a dowser friend, he drew my attention to four stones, set in the turf behind an old croft ruin, each stone about 20 centimetres across and set about five or six metres apart. His pendulum indicated that these stones were active, and my Oasis Rod showed that there was a line running through them, although this was not an area in which I believed there was a ley line.

I thought a lot about this phenomenon when I got home, and decided to try an experiment. Having found a part of the lawn in front of my house where the Oasis Rod indicated that there were no lines present, I set out four of my male-charged stones in a line, about three metres apart from each other. Testing with my Oasis Rod, I found a line apparently similar to a ley line running between them. Moreover, this line continued at each end beyond the outermost stones. These outer parts of the line were a complete mystery, since I had been careful to set out the line of stones so that it did not point at any object on which it would be likely to attach itself.

I had apparently created my first ley line, and I quickly removed the stones so that this line could not possibly contaminate the environment. I decided, however, that this phenomenon must be investigated in much greater detail.

# 4.
# Measuring the Charge

Unfortunately, the existence of ley lines is not recognized by orthodox science, which requires that a phenomenon must be both measurable and repeatable if it is to be considered as part of reality, although this is, of course, no longer strictly true in the sub-atomic world. So far no instrument has been designed that will react to the energy thought to be transmitted along these ley lines; so it has not been possible to satisfy the first of these conditions. It has always seemed to me that this is no cause for denying their existence, since it may only be the ineptitude of the scientist in that he has not so far been clever enough to design suitable apparatus.

There are certain grounds for believing that Wilhelm Reich had gone a long way in his researches into this form of energy, which he called Orgone, and was well on the way to making such measurements.[21] Unfortunately, in the early 1940s, the public administration of the United States was not convinced of his claims, and he was thrown into prison, where he died shortly after, and most of his research papers were publicly burnt. More recently, Dr Don Robins has been able to demonstrate ultra-sonic activity at dawn round the Rollright Stones in Oxfordshire,[20] this being part of the Dragon Project organized by *The Ley Hunter* magazine. Although I consider these findings most valuable in that they indicate some form of energy activity around these megalithic monuments, I do not feel that these observations can be considered as measurements of the ley lines themselves, but rather as an epiphenomenon originating from the activity in these stones.

It had occured to me, when I had been working on the dating of imprinted stones,[8] as I described above, that I could possibly use the radius of gyration of the pendulum as a measurement of the energy stored in these stones. The big objection to this was that dowsing is considered by orthodox science, even if it is acknowledged to exist at all, to be a highly subjective phenomenon that is not repeatable. This, I am certain, is taking too strict a view of repeatability, and is based on the nineteenth-century dogma of the physical sciences that all factors other than the one being studied must be eliminated, so that any reaction observed must have been caused by the one variant being examined.

During my career as an agricultural scientist I had been accustomed to carrying out experiments on crops in an environment that was quite outside my control. Indeed, experiments carried out in a controlled environment, for example in a glass-house, with uniform soil and weather conditions etc., would give little indication of the performance of the crop in the field. Thus it is of no use applying the treatment to one half of a field, leaving the other half untreated as a 'control', and then comparing the yields from the two halves of the crop; weather and soil conditions may have been quite different on either half and the difference in yield may not therefore be due to the treatment given. However, during the early years of the present century fundamental pioneer work was done at Rothamsted Experimental Station by Professor R. A. Fisher on the techniques of statistical analysis, which was to lead to enormous advances in agricultural science.

Fisher showed that, if a field experiment was laid out on strictly controlled lines, usually in the form of randomized blocks within which each of the treatments was replicated, it was possible to analyse the resulting yields in such a way that the effects of each of the various factors affecting the yields could be separated. In fact, what one gets is a variation in yield for each treatment given in each block, and by the mathematical technique known as Analysis of Variance it is possible to assign what proportion of the variance in yield is due to such factors as soil differences, wind exposure etc., as well as to the treatments applied. When each of these assigned variances is subtracted from the total variance in yield, one is left with a residue known as error, which is due to all the smaller factors affecting the crop that one has not been able to identify. Finally, one has to consider whether the effects of the treatment one has given to the crop are real or probably due to chance. This is done by comparing them with the residual error and expressing the ratio in terms of probability. What one accepts as real is purely subjective, but for agricultural experiments anything less than a probability of 1 in 20 ($P = 0.05$) that one's original hypothesis is due to chance is generally considered as satisfactory. This means that, if one advises twenty farmers to carry out such a treatment, one can reasonably expect nineteen of them to be successful. I have, however, had on more than one occasion, the difficult task of trying to convince an irate twentieth farmer, whom I had advised to follow my recommendations, that I was not totally incompetent and that he was merely unlucky!

Another most useful statistical technique, which I was able to use in dowsing, was the Analysis of Covariance. If one suspects that a factor A is varying with a second factor B, one plots these as a graph and tries to draw a line through the resulting points to illustrate this relationship. Assuming that the resulting line is straight, one can, by subjecting the data to an Analysis of Covariance, find the best possible straight line that can be drawn through these points and also estimate the probability of this relationship being real. The more mathematical reader will, of course, point out that the relationship being studied may not be direct, i.e. a straight line. It might, for example, be inverse or exponential, etc. With experience, however, after the preliminary plotting it is possible to spot the sort of relationship one is dealing with and to apply what is known as a Transformation. Thus, if the relationship is inverse, one uses the reciprocal of the factor B, and if exponential the logarithm.

Using statistical techniques of this type, I found it was quite possible to use the 'unreliable' art of dowsing to make repeatable measurements to a degree of probability that would have been quite acceptable, at least to an agricultural scientist. I very much doubt, however, if such a measuring technique would be acceptable to a hard-core physical scientist. More than once in my scientific career I have used an unorthodox method of measurement based on observation of biological reactions, only to have the research report rejected by the editor of a scientific journal on the grounds that the referees, to whom he had sent the typescript, considered that the technique used was unreliable. This proved particularly irritating when similar findings were published some ten years afterwards by another worker using a more 'physical' method evolved later.

If I was to use the radius of gyration of the pendulum as a measure of the power in these stones and lines I had first to design some means of accurately estimating the radius. In the article in the *Journal* of the British Society of Dowsers,[11] where I outlined this work, I described and figured a 'gyrometer' for use in the field. Most of the work to be described here was, however, carried out in the more peaceful atmosphere inside my former church, and a simpler gyrometer was used. This consisted of a scale of centimetres marked on a strip of card, with 0 at the centre and 25 at each end. This was fixed about 15 centimetres from the floor, and a parallel beam of light focused on it. The stone or line to be measured was arranged to be about 20 centimetres in front of the scale, and the pendulum was held over it so that the shadow of the bob was just below the scale on the card (Figure 6). As the pendulum gyrated, the shadow of the cord appeared to move back and forth over the scale, and, when it had settled down to a steady rhythm, the radius of gyration could be read off the scale to the nearest half-centimetre.

I had already noticed that the longer the cord (rate) the larger the radius of gyration appeared to be. I therefore tried dividing each radius of gyration as measured by the length of the card used, for a number of materials, using the appropriate Lethbridge rate. I found that whatever the material used, at any one time, I obtained the same figure. I therefore called this the Standard Swing ($S_s/R$). Unfortunately, I further discovered that if I repeated these measurements at another time I obtained a different figure for this ratio. The problem was,

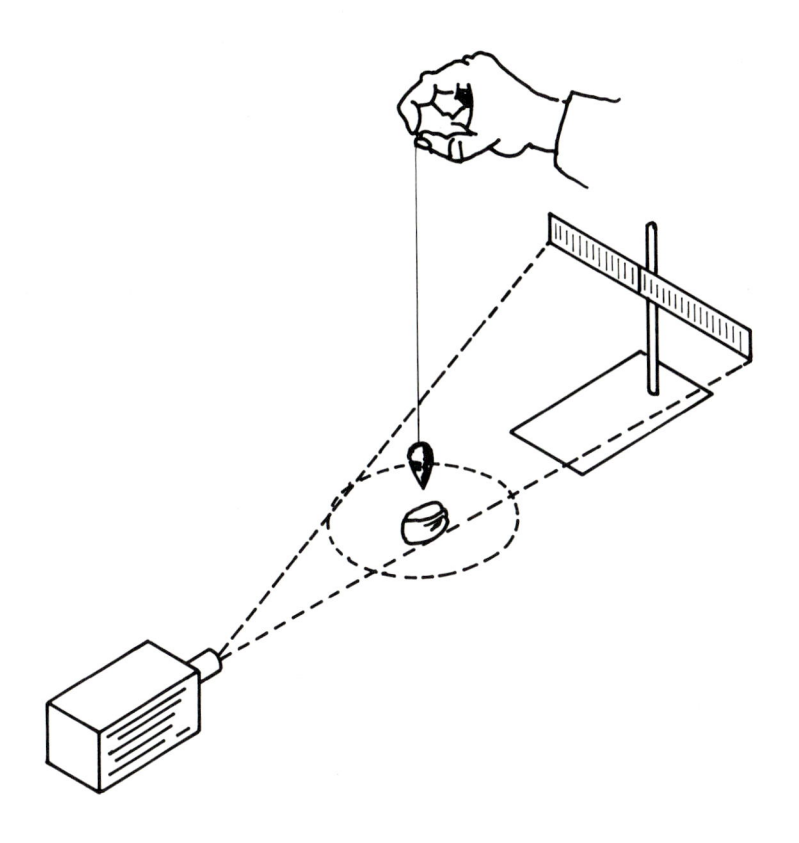

Figure 6. Gyrometer for measuring charge with a pendulum.

therefore, to discover how this figure varied with time and whether it could be predicted with any certainty. I need not confuse the general reader with the details of this inquiry, which I reported fully in an article in the *Journal of the British Society of Dowsers*, and which I have brought fully up-to-date in Appendix A. In short, I found that these variations were controlled by a factor I called Psi ($\psi$), which itself appeared to vary with the phases of the moon and some form of daily rhythm. This Psi factor was related to a measure that Lethbridge[13] used to determine the psychic potential of an individual. Using a pendulum with a cord 22.5cm long, he counted the number of revolutions it made before returning to an oscillatory movement.

Having thus a standard for comparison, I could now compare this with the radius of gyration observed $S_o/R$) with the pendulum held over a charged stone, and I called the ratio of these two swings the charge on that particular stone. This charge I measured in units which I called petrons (see Glossary). In practice, I found that the charge ranged from around 20 petrons, where it was barely measureable with the pendulum, to figures up to nearly 200 petrons. Detailed study over a large number of measurements indicates that I could obtain by this technique figures which were likely to have an error of not more than ± 3 per cent.

I recently discussed this method of quantitative measurement with the long pendulum with a philosopher friend and some rather interesting conclusions were reached. There seem to be good reasons for believing that dowsing with the long pendulum may differ fundamentally from dowsing with the short pendulum. As I have mentioned before, when using the short pendulum one can only obtain the answers 'Yes/No/Don't know', and therefore to make quantitative measurements certain subterfuges have to be adopted. For example, if one wants to know the depth at which water occurs at a certain site, one then has to ask such a question as: 'Does water occur here at over 350 feet?' If the pendulum gyrates, indicating a positive answer, one then goes on to ask: 'Does it occur at over 450 feet?' Should the pendulum now oscillate indicating 'No', one then reduces the figure to, say, 400 feet and so on until the margin is small enough for one's purpose at this site. Thus, the conscious mind is directing certain specific questions to the subconscious, which replies through the medium of the pendulum with the answers 'Yes' or 'No'.

An alternative method of questioning the short pendulum was described by me when outlining my method of dating.[8] As mentioned earlier, this used the binary notation of 'Yes or not yes'. Again, it is asking a specific question of 'Is this number, of which I am thinking (i.e. one of the binary series 1, 2, 4, 8, etc.) a component of the date of this object?', and receiving an answer from the pendulum. But, because the total is not some indication of the charge in the stone.

# 5.
# The Charge in Stones

I now had an acceptably repeatable means of measuring the charge, indicated by the pendulum, in both the charged stones and also in ley lines. Since I had noted earlier that a line, in all respects similar to a ley line, ran between two adjacent charged stones, it seemed a good idea that I should first investigate this charge in the stones and then go on to study the lines between them.

To recapitulate what I had already found and outlined in Chapter 1: a stone could be charged by holding it in the hand and hammering or throwing it hard at a neutral wall; but, if the stone was not handled, neither throwing nor hammering imprinted a charge. Moreover, hammering an uncharged stone alongside one that was already charged imparted into it a similar charge. Having now the means of evaluating these charges, I was able to measure that of both the 'parent' and the 'daughter' stones, and found that they were not significantly different, bearing in mind the error I was likely to encounter when using this measuring technique. For example, stone No. 6 had been heavily hammered in my hand and showed a charge of 122.2 petrons. On placing the unhandled stone No. 18 alongside stone 6 and hammering it in an area where I could detect no other charge, I found that stone 18 had acquired a charge of 120.5, i.e. well within the predicted error of ± 9 per cent.

If a charge could be transferred by placing two stones

## THE CHARGE IN STONES

together and then fixing it by hammering, how far apart could they be for this still to occur? To test this, I hammered a number of stones, each a little further from the 'parent' stone. From these I discovered that a similar charge was imparted to a stone as long as it was within a radius of 60 cm round a male parent stone; outside this circle no charge was imparted from the parent stone. It will be recalled that Lethbridge had discovered that the base of the cone rising above a charged object had a radius equal to that of the rate of the charge. From my experiments it was clear that any unhandled stone placed within this cone was becoming charged and that this could be made permanent by hammering. To check this conclusion, I repeated the experiment with a female-charged stone and found that it transferred a similar charge to unhandled stones as long as they were within a radius of 72.5 cm, i.e. the female rate.

If this charge existed only within the cone or field round a charged stone, was this also true of the wedge-shaped area of the parallels on either side of a line? It will be recalled from Chapter 2 that I had found a male line running down the centre of my church building, with parallel lines on either side, and that these and the female lines at the sides of the church did not run at floor level, the widest part of the wedge being at the height of the eaves. Only at this height were the parallels on either side of the main lines at a distance equal to the rate; at floor level they were somewhat closer. I had, therefore, to allow for this, when placing my stones to be hammered. A measurement of the strength of this line with the gyrometer gave a figure of 120.5. I then placed an untouched stone just within the parallel distance from where I believed the central line to be, and another just outside this range. After hammering both stones, their charge was measured in the usual way, with the result that the stone which had been within the parallels had a charge of 121.1; that on the outside had no detectable charge. There was also the female line in the church running down the sides under the edge of the gallery. I was, therefore, able to repeat this experiment with this line, and found that only the stone hammered within the parallels received the charge.

These experiments indicated the useful fact that I had

within the church certain areas where there was either a male or female line, on which I could charge stones by placing them near by and hammering them to fix it. Also — and this was to prove very useful — there appeared to be neutral areas between these lines and within the church where no charge was imparted to an unhandled stone. But, as will be seen later, matters were not quite as simple as they appeared at this time to be, and difficulties arose when I came to consider lines between charged stones and parts of the church wall. I shall be dealing with this particular problem in the church in more detail in a later chapter. It also appeared that the outside of the church walls carried no detectable charge — otherwise unhandled stones thrown at them would have become charged. There was one other mystery: handled stones thrown at the wall received a charge that was fixed when they hit the wall, although they were outside my immediate field when this blow was received. This seemed to suggest that the charge imparted by handling was retained long enough, while travelling through the air from me to the wall, to become fixed in full on striking the wall.

It may well be wondered how I managed to do all this without handling the stones. In fact, what I had done was to make a pair of long wooden tongs, which I always used for picking up the stones I did not wish to handle. This kept them well out of my personal field, and with a little practice I was able to use these tongs to throw stones at the church walls. At a later date, I found an old pair of iron fire-tongs nearly three feet long and discovered that these were invaluable for moving stones about the place without handling them and thus imparting a charge. As will be described later, I found that to neither wood nor iron is it possible to impart a charge, so that both pairs of tongs remained neutral even after long use.

To investigate this problem of stone-throwing, I handled a number of stones, immediately threw one of them at the church wall and then measured with the gyrometer the charge fixed in it. The other stones were kept in an uncharged area, picked up with the wooden tongs, and thrown at the wall after various lengths of time. The charges fixed in these stones were then measured in a similar manner. The charge of each of these stones, expressed as a percentage of the full charge, i.e.

that of the first stone, was then plotted as a graph against time elapsed since handling. This showed that there was indeed a steady loss in charge, which appeared to be exponential in form. The percentage charge was, therefore, replotted against the logarithm of the time elapsed since handling, and a good straight line was obtained. This indicated a half-life averaging log 2.25 minutes, i.e. just about three hours. In other words, after this period of time the charge would drop to 50 per cent of what it had been immediately after handling; after another three hours it would have dropped to 25 per cent, and after twenty-four hours it would be less than 0.4 per cent, i.e. it would then be quite undetectable.

I wondered whether the length of time the stone was held in the hand had any effect on this decay time. I therefore carried round stones for periods of 5, 30, 60 and 120 minutes and then tested them in the same way for decay rates. I was surprised to find that none of this made the slightest difference, and that the charge in each case still decayed at the same rate of 50 per cent in three hours. In desperation I carried this experiment to extreme lengths and carried a small stone about in my pocket, where it was frequently handled, over a period of several weeks. However, on measuring the charge 24 hours after I had removed the stone from my pocket, and without touching it again, all detectable charge had evaporated. It therefore appears that simple handling, even with a strong desire, is not sufficient to fix a charge in a stone. I found it difficult to believe, however, that blows with a hammer or against a neutral wall, are the only means of fixing this charge into stones. I could hardly believe that the stones I had found charged on primitive graves — as described in Chapter 1 — had all been beaten with a hammer or thrown on to the grave with some considerable force.

I thought, therefore, that I had better look into this question of how the charge was fixed in stones. My first attempt was to see if I could remove a charge already fixed in a stone. To do this, I charged a small stone by hammering it in my hand and then measured the resulting charge. I then placed this stone in my sitting-room fire, where it remained all night. In the morning its charge was again measured and found to be the same as before. Having discovered that heat could not remove a charge already fixed in a stone, I now had to find out if it could fix a charge already implanted. To test this I collected three stones from the beach and handled all three of them. Stone A was then hammered to fix this charge; stone B was placed in the fire and left there all night; stone C was set aside and not handled further. The following morning, without handling any of these stones, I measured their charges with the gyrometer, finding that stones A and B had a charge of 151.3, while in stone C I could detect no charge whatever. Thus, if stone B had not been heated in the fire, its charge would have decayed, as it had in stone C, hence proving that heating is an effective method of fixing a charge. This fact explains why there is usually a charge to be found fixed in pottery, particularly if it is handmade, since firing the clay would fix the potter's field into the pottery. Machine-made ceramics are more variable, and this would seem to indicate that the period between handling and firing may have allowed any acquired charge to decay.

Aubrey Burl[i] and many other archaeologists have described finding the remains of cremated bodies at the base of standing stones, together with reddish soil indicating the heat caused by the cremation. There have been many and various suggestions as to why megalithic man carried out this practice, but the fact that heat fixes the charge on stone suggests a reason which at least is open to experimental testing.

If a body is simply buried at the base of a standing stone it is clear that, if close enough, its charge will be imparted to the stone, but in time the body will decay and, as shown in Chapter 1, the charge will ultimately be lost. Probably early megalithic man found that he could impart a charge to a standing stone by burying a body at its base, but being then ignorant of the techniques for fixing this charge, he found it gradually faded away, leaving the stone uncharged. Later, when he was familiar with the means of fixing a charge, he would have discovered that cremating the body at the base of the stone would fix the charge into the soil and this would be permanently imparted to the stone standing in this soil. Thus, if he was using an unworked stone, to which no charge had been imparted by hammering, he would still be able to obtain a permanent charge.

Heat as a means of fixing the charge also raises a rather interesting speculation. I have mentioned finding a number of centres when I was ley hunting, which had the appearance of being beacon sites where ceremonies at the feast of Beltane may have taken place. Many writers have described how, at these ceremonies, young men and women used to jump through the beacon fires which they had lit. Now, if it were desired to fix a sex charge into the rock at the top of a hill, one could obviously not stand near enough to the fire for this to be effective. As an alternative to burning some sacrifice at the stake, a field could be continually passed over the fire and thus be fixed to the rock by the heat generated by the beacon, without danger to the participants.

While on the subject of folk lore, it is interesting to speculate that the fixing of a charge by blows may be a possible explanation for the ancient custom of 'beating the parish bounds'. Writers have described how the priest and choirboys went round the parish boundary beating the ground with rods. (I believe that in some parishes this practice has degenerated into beating the choirboys. Although this may well have been justified, it would not have any lasting effect on the parish boundaries). Beating the ground would, however, fix the personal charge of the priest on that line and would, in times when most people were sensitive dowsers, be obvious to any interloper coming into the territory. This practice, therefore, closely resembles the habit of many animals marking out the boundaries of their territory with their urine or other scent. If the ground was stony rather than rocky, the charged stones would tend to be scattered during cultivation or building, and hence the line would have to be marked out again each year by the appropriate ceremony.

Dr Ron Robins[20] has suggested that this property of stones to absorb some form of charge from a field may be due to the free electrons found in quartz rocks becoming fixed in the crystal lattice. I am not competent fully to understand this theory, but it seemed to me that, if it is correct, perhaps an electromagnet would fix a charge already imparted to a stone. I therefore placed a handled stone on an electromagnet and left it there for three days. If the magnet was having no effect, the charge in this stone should have decayed so that it was no longer detectable after this period. On removing the stone, without further handling, I measured the charge, and was delighted to find that it was still fully present. Just to make sure, I measured it again after a period of some weeks and found the full charge still present.

I thus had another method of fixing the charge into stones. Was this, perhaps, the means by which standing stones became charged? Tom Graves[12] has suggested that standing stones were placed by megalithic man over blind springs and that at these points the Earth's cosmic charge rose to the surface. Certainly, all standing stones I have examined are sited over blind springs, and, if these are electromagnetic in character, a charge could possibly have been fixed in them by this means.

On thinking over all this, I wondered whether, if an electromagnet could fix a charge in a stone, it could perhaps also induce one into an unhandled stone. I therefore placed an unhandled stone on the magnet and left it there for three days. On removing it, again without handling, I tested it with the pendulum, but I could detect no sign of a charge. The electromagnet can, therefore, fix a charge induced by other means, but cannot itself induce one.

Whatever other means of fixing the charge in stones might be available, in this study I was using blows of a hammer, etc., and it seemed desirable to assess the amount of force required to fix a full charge. So far, using stones averaging just over 100 grams in weight, I had been hitting them ten times fairly hard with the hammer. The force exerted by a hammer blow cannot, however, easily be measured or remain uniform over a long series. I decided, therefore, to use a stone of known weight dropped from a known height on to the specimen stone placed in a steady and known field, i.e. the central line in the church.

In the first series of this experiment I used specimen stones each weighing about 100 grams. One stone was hammered ten times and used to assess the full power of the field. On the remaining stones, another stone weighing 260g was dropped from heights of 5, 10, 15, 20, and 25 or 30 inches respectively. The resulting charge fixed in each was then measured with the gyrometer, after allowing time for decay of any excess charge. The results showed that, for stones of this size, a weight of 260g had to be dropped from a height of about 28 inches to fix the full power of the field.

On considering these results, I realized that it was difficult to draw any general conclusions from this because the stone is not falling at a uniform speed but is accelerating (at 981 cm per second per second). I therefore tried a second series, this time allowing the stone to fall from a uniform height of 15 inches in each case and varying the nubmer of blows from one to four. From this I gathered that a stone of about 114g had to receive a minimum of four blows from a weight of 260g dropped from a height of 15 inches to fix the full charge of the field. Did these figures hold for stones of greater weight? So far I had been working with mere pebbles, whereas what I was really interested in was how a charge could be fixed in standing stones perhaps weighing up to a thousand or more times as much as my pebbles.

In my next experiment I used a heavier weight, i.e. 751g, dropped from a uniform height of 20cm, on to ten stones of weights varying from 120g to just over 4.5 kilos, placed on the church central line. The charge fixed in each of these stones was later measured with the gyrometer, and the results were plotted as percentages of the full charge of the field, against the weight of the stone. This indicated that there was, in fact, a steady fall in the percentage of full charge fixed as the weight of the stones increased.

The results of these experiments can be expressed in a variety of ways, e.g. that the amount of work required to fix a charge of 120 petrons into a stone weighing 1 kilo is equivalent to 0.15kg. However, what we have to imagine is a megalithic stonemason sitting astride a lump of rock which he is trying to shape into a form suitable for a standing stone. He is doing this with the only means available to him — a stone hand-axe weighing, say, 750 grams. Since the boulder is well within his personal field, how many times does he have to strike with the hand-axe from a height of, say, 25 centimetres, to fix the full charge of his field into the completed stone?

To extrapolate the above results to a standing stone, first we have to know the approximate weight of the completed stone.

Obviously, a direct measurement of the weight would be a task well outside my available equipment. If, however, the specific gravity of the stone is known and its approximate volume, the weight can be easily calculated. I remembered from my school physics lessons that all one had to do was to weigh a sample of the stone in air and then again when immersed in water; on comparing these two weights, one has a figure for the specific gravity. Nearly all the standing stones in my locality are constructed from Torridonian Sandstone or Lewisian Gneiss. I therefore collected three samples of each, with differing grain sizes in case this affected the results, and weighed them in air and then in water, obtaining mean specific gravities of 2.599 for the Torridonian Sandstone and 2.499 for the Gneiss.

I decided to measure the standing stone lying just above my house, which happens to be of Lewisian Gneiss, but this proved no easy task owing to is peculiar shape. It is a typical pointed stone of four-sided cross section, but none of the four sides are of the same dimension, and the slope to the apex is not uniform. However, by taking plenty of measurements and making some calculations, I decided that it has a volume of about 0.15 cubic metres. Multiplying this by 2.499, the specific gravity of Gneiss, I obtained a figure of about 375 kilos. From the above calculations it is clear that one would have to strike this stone some 428 times with a hand-axe of 750g to imprint the full charge of one's personal field. This standing stone is admittedly of a very modest size, but, if our mason has been exerting any extra degree of muscular power into his blows, it is clear that the work required to fix the charge would have been well inside the amount needed to shape this stone even if he had been very skilled.

The so-called 'lawn' of my garden has a number of large boulders in it, which rise just above the general level of the surrounding grass and form a considerable hazard to the mower. During warm summer afternoons I have often spent a few hours trying to reduce the tops of these boulders by no more than an inch or two, using a steel bolster and a two-pound hammer. Admittedly, my efforts are very unskilled compared with our hypothetical Stone Age mason, but I have found it takes many blows to remove a most paltry amount of stone, even with this more sophisticated equipment.

# THE CHARGE IN STONES

When one considers the very large size of the Sarsen Stones of Stonehenge, which are, I believe, estimated to weigh up to 50 tons, one realizes that the amount of work entailed in shaping them to a roughly rectangular form, with the mortise and tenon on the top shaped to receive the lintel stones, must have been enormous. On the other hand, it would have taken some 50,000 blows with a stone axe to fix the charge of a worker's field. This sounds a great deal, but I have found that one can, with an easy rhythm, give one such blow per second; so the required number of blows could be given in just under fourteen hours work. I cannot believe that these huge stones could have been shaped in such a short time as this with such primitive equipment.

An even larger stone is the Grand Menhir Brisé at Carnac. The Thoms[22] describe this stone as having been about 70 feet high when it was upright and in one piece, and weighing about 300 tons. They suggest that it must have been cut from the solid rock by the making of trenches, 10-12 feet deep, with stone hammers, wedges, and water. Using the above data to calculate the work required to fix the charge of a worker's field into this immense stone, one gets a figure of 300,000 blows; at one per second, this represents a period of little over 83 man-hours, a quite trifling fraction of the physical work that it must have taken to cut out this stone.

To check these ideas, I selected the largest boulder I could conveniently handle and weighed it on the bathroom scales — admittedly a rather crude method, but the best I could do with a stone of this size. I found that it weighed about 4 stone 6lb (about 28 kilos). Using the hand-held stone weighing 750g and beating it on the church central line, I calculated that it would require some 32 strokes to fix the full charge of about 130 petrons. If, however, I gave it the full 32 strokes — and this proved to be more than was actually required — I would still only get a figure of the full charge. I therefore decided to give it 24 strokes to give an estimated 75 per cent of the full charge. At the same time I beat a small stone 12 times to give me a figure for the full charge of the line at the time of the experiment. This latter gave a figure of 133.9 petrons. Before the charge in the larger stone could be measured at least 24 hours had to elapse so that the excess charge picked up on the line could decay. To make certain of this, I left it for three days and then measured the remaining charge with the gyrometer, getting a figure of 108.6 petrons or 81 per cent of the full charge. This would seem to indicate that I had been exerting some slight muscular power in excess of a falling stone, and that a

Figure 7. Dream scene of charging a standing stone.

reasonable figure would have been one stroke of the stone hammer to fix the charge in each kilo of a standing stone.

Hammering, heat and an electromagnetic field may not, however, be the only means of fixing a charge in a standing stone. Early in 1977 I had been re-reading J. W. Dunne's *Experiment with Time* and kept a record of my dreams over a period of about three months. One night I had a clear and unusual dream. I appeared to be standing on the left of a valley running between rounded hills. At the head of this valley was a circular wall surrounding a tall, white stone, which somewhat resembled a lighthouse (Figure 7). Round the wall was a line of people dressed in what appeared to be early seventeenth-century fashions, i.e. the men in short, black tunics, rather baggy breeches and hose, white collars and tall hats; the women in long skirts, white shawls, and caps. I had the impression, although I could not actually see anything, that they were passing something round in an anti-clockwise direction. There was a gap in the wall facing down the valley, and, after some time, something seemed to issue from this gap and rush down the valley with a sound rather like escaping steam or a sudden rush of wind. This rushed past me down the valley, although I could not actually see anything. At this point I woke up and recorded the dream in my diary.

I would not care to think what the Freudian interpretation of this dream might be, but my own explanation, for what it is worth, is that I had witnessed a ceremony of charging a stone. The early seventeenth century was, of course, a time of considerable spread of witchcraft, particularly in Scotland, where it was much condemned by James VI in his *Daemonologie*. It is known that there was a ritual called the 'raising of the power', although I have no idea of the details of this. Could it possibly have been some method of raising the group's collective psi count, and of in some way transferring this to the stone in the centre of the circular wall?

To check on this idea that the psi count of a person was related to the charge on a stone placed in their field, I hammered five stones in my hand, one every two hours on a day of full moon. The results are shown in Figure 8, where it will be seen that there is a good relationship between the charge fixed in these stones and the value of my psi count at

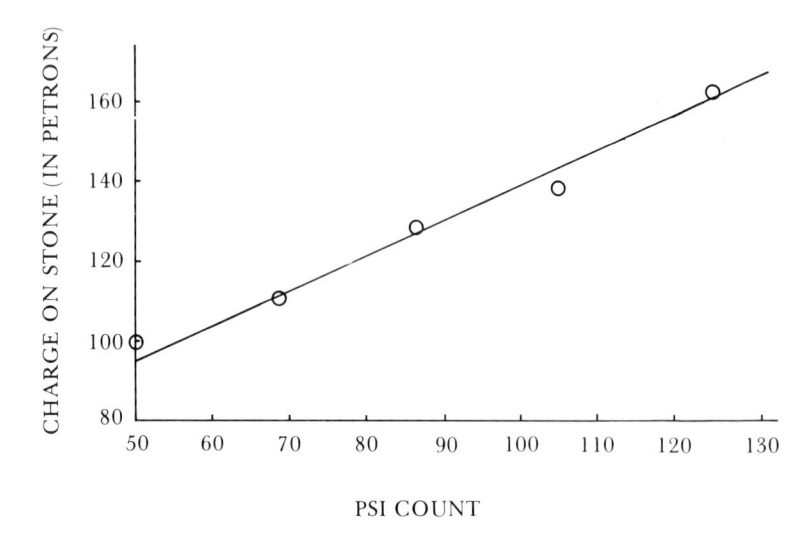

Figure 8. Effect of personal psi count on charge of a hand-held stone.

the time the stones were held in my hand and hammered.

It is of interest to note that the highest charge I was able to fix in a stone was 162 petrons, and that this was at the time of full moon, a time notorious for witchcraft activity. Admittedly, it was at 4 p.m. and not midnight, as one might have expected. No doubt an experienced witch would be able to 'raise the power' to a much higher level than this; but this is the highest value I have been able to fix into a stone by means of my personal field. There is, however, an alternative and rather different interpretation of what I thought I was observing in this dream, and I shall deal with this in a later chapter.

Before leaving the subject of charging a single stone, there is one further aspect that should be considered. So far I had been dealing solely with stones either of Torridonian Sandstone, Lewisian Gneiss, or occasionally Quartzite. I was interested to see what other substances could be induced to take up a male or female charge.

Lethbridge pointed out that most, if not all, organic material, such as that from plants, shells and bones from animals, etc., already had their own sex charge inherent in them, and that a further charge of opposite polarity could not then be induced. Although my own observations were far from extensive, I was able to confirm this. Man-made organic material — such as plastics — has no inherent sex charge, nor can one be induced in it. Inorganic materials, such as metals, also have no inherent sex charge, but such a charge can usually be induced in them in the same way as I had induced it into stones. A possible explanation that occured to me is that such inorganic materials are usually crystalline in structure, whereas plant and animal material is usually amorphous. Establishing whether or not such an explanation is sound needs for more investigation than I have been able to give it, and it is anyway outside the scope of present study, which is primarily concerned with the origin and nature of ley lines.

Another aspect of the sex charge, discussed by Lethbridge on a number of occasions, was the phenomenon of 'interrupters'. He found that certain materials, e.g. some forms of iron, graphite, common salt, and woods such as elm and elder, had the property of 'masking' the sex charge in an adjoining material, or even of changing its polarity. This is quite an intriguing phenomenon, and, although I was able to use it later when studying lines between stones, it is one which I have not as yet been able to examine in any great depth.

An inherent charge in a material is not transferable to another substance, even when beaten together. Thus, placing a stone on a sheet of copper and hammering it with an iron hammer, did not transfer the rates for copper (76cm) or iron (80cm) to the stone. The two sex rates, therefore, appear to be somewhat different in character from other rates, although perhaps Lethbridge's rates for more abstract concepts, such as courage or anger, may be of similar form.

# 6.
# Lines and the Charge in Stones

I now had a fair idea of how, and why, stones became fixed with this mysterious charge, and it seemed to be time that I should start looking at the relation between two adjoining stones and the resultant line running between them when they were separated.

First, I thought I should try to understand what happened when two charged stones were placed together, i.e. when the distance between them was zero. I therefore gathered together a fair selection of stones with fixed charges, mainly male, varying in charge from about 20 to about 160 petrons, and in weight from 70 grams to 4½ kilos. I selected two, placed them together, and then measured the combined charge with the gyrometer. This was repeated with a number of other pairs of stones of varying weight and charge.

Having collected a reasonable body of data, I tried to see if I could make any sense of it. I thought that one of three alternative explanations might be possible: (a) the combined charge would be the sum of that of the two stones, although this seemed unlikely; (b) it would be the mean of the two; or (c) it would be something quite different, and more complicated. On considering the results I had obtained so far, I was dismayed to find that it was clear that neither explanation (a) nor (b) would fit the case. The resulting charge certainly lay between those of the two stones concerned, but it tended to be closer to that of the larger stone; only when the two stones were of equal weight did the charge coincide with the mean.

After much thought I decided to put forward the following hypothetical equation and see if this would fit the results I had obtained:

$$C_0 = \frac{(C_1 \times M_1) + (C_2 \times M_2)}{M_1 + M_2} \quad \ldots \ldots 6(1)$$

Most people with a non-mathematical mind are inclined to look at an equation, however simple, and go completely blank. I will therefore try to explain this one, and the reasoning behind it, in simple terms.

$C_0$ is the joint charge on the pair of stones at zero separation, which is what we are trying to measure with the pendulum and gyrometer. $C_1$ and $C_2$ are the respective charges of the two stones with which we are working, and which we have previously measured. $M_1$ and $M_2$ are their weights (mass) expressed in kilos. The numerator (upper part of the fraction, above the line) is made up of the charge multiplied by the weight for each stone, and these are then added together. This quantity (C x M) I decided to call the 'power' of the stone, measured in units of 100 termed 'lithons'. Thus, a stone of 1 kilo and a charge of 100 petrons, would have a power of 1 lithon. However, it is the combined charge of the two stones that we are measuring with the gyrometer; so the sum of the two powers has to be divided by the sum of the two masses ($M_1 + M_2$). This is not, of course, the same as dividing each power by its own mass, when one would then simply get the sum of the two charges — which, as we have already seen, is not the right answer.

Now, with this equation and the known charge and mass of each stone I was using, I was able to calculate a charge for the two together and compare this with the result I had obtained with the gyrometer and pendulum. This I did and found that the calculated charge certainly related very well with the observed one, except that it was nearly always about 10 per cent less. I was quite unable to see any reason for this discrepancy and went on measuring pairs of stones and calculating their theoretical combined charge for a period of about three months, quite without any further elucidation. In desperation I finally got tired of this and decided to go on to the next stage without solving this problem, using the calculated figure for zero separation, rather than that actually measured.

This next stage was, in fact, to move the two stones apart and to see what was the 'strength' of the line between them at various distances of separation. I decided to call this the strength of the line rather than the charge, which did not seem very appropriate for a line. The strength was, however, being measured in the same way as charge, i.e. with the gyrometer; so, rightly or wrongly, I stuck to the same units of petrons.

Previous to starting the work on paired stones I had been doing most of this work in the vestry, a small room, about nine feet square, at the north-west end of the church. I now had to have more room to spread out my two stones; so I moved on to the eastern gallery. I had already checked that there were no detectable lines running along this gallery, and it gave me a stretch of more than fifty feet to spread out my stones. I therefore set up two stones about twenty feet apart on this gallery and duly checked with both pendulum and Oasis Rod that there was a line between them. I then tested the space between each end wall and the nearest stone, and was discouraged to find that there was a line here also. There had been no line between these walls before, but when I set up these two stones, a line appeared from wall to wall. I then recalled the experiment I had tried at the outset of this work, namely, setting up four stones in line in the garden and finding a line between them as well as weak lines running out from each end-stone. It would appear that, when one sets up a line between two stones, this line continues and 'latches on' to the nearest suitable object, i.e. some charged object.

I thought I would check this idea and see what would happen if there was no suitable target for the line to latch on to. Looking out north-west from the Rhu-na-Bidh point over Loch Shieldaig, there is a gap about 1km wide between the points of Ardheslaig and Diabaig. To the left of this gap, the tops of the hills of Harris and South Lewis, some fifty miles away, can be seen on a clear day, but to the right all land is below the sea horizon. On the point of Rhu-na-Bidh I set out two stones, each of about 1½ kilos in weight, with a charge of 120 and 114 respectively. The seaward stone was about 1 metre from the edge of the cliff, and the other about 6 metres further inland. The line between them was carefully sited to run to the horizon where no land could be seen. Between the stones there was a line with a strength of just over 100 petrons as measured with the portable gyrometer, and inland, a line of 52 petrons. I could detect nothing with the pendulum on the seaward side. I then moved the inland stone so that the line was pointing to the highest part of the Ardheslaig peninsula, which is just about 4 km distant. I could now just detect a line on the seaward side, with a swing of the pendulum of only 2 cm radius, indicating a strength of 17.5 petrons. I am not sure what features there may be on the Ardheslaig peninsula, since I have not yet surveyed it; but I do know that several ley lines run out in its direction, and there are in all probability several standing stones in that area.

This all seemed to show that, if one sets up a line between two stones, the line will extend at both ends when there is something suitable for it to latch on to. With my line on the gallery of the church, the end walls were forming a suitable target. As I stated above, I had been unable to detect any line running along the gallery **before** I had placed the two stones there, and I had assumed, wrongly, that the walls were not charged, especially as I had picked up no charge when throwing stones at the outside. This conclusion must have been wrong, since the outside of the church is constructed of squared stones, which would have picked up a charge from the masons shaping them. On the other hand, the inner part of the walls, which are over a metre thick, is formed of rubble and plaster, which would not have been charged. The charge of the cut stones would therefore, have to be shared with the rubble, considerably reducing the overall power. The interesting point is that the only indication of this charge was the male and female lines running down the inside of the church length, as I have previously described. We shall have to consider this problem further in the next chapter.

Whatever the reasons for all this, I had to find some way of isolating my two-stone line so that it was not interfered with by the power of the church walls. Migrating to the garden would not help, because I would then find the line latching on to all kinds of unknown objects in the environment! My mind, therefore, turned to Lethbridge's interrupters, mentioned in the last chapter. I wondered whether a sheet of iron placed at each end of the gallery would stop the church interferring. I collected a pair of old tin trays, placed one at either end of the gallery, and again set up my two stones. The reader can imagine my relief when I could detect no line between these stones and the walls, only that between the two stones!

After some thought I wondered if this interference by the church walls was the cause of my previous trouble with the combined charge of two stones at zero separation. I thought, therefore, I would try measuring this joint charge with the two stones isolated from external effects. I had in the meantime found that fine gauge (30mm or less) wire-netting was just as good an interrupter as sheet iron; so I surrounded my two stones with this at a distance of about a metre and measured the joint charge. On comparing this with the figure I had obtained with the unscreened stones, I found a reduction in charge of 8.8 per cent. I repeated this with other pairs of stones and found very similar figures of reduction. The interference by the church walls had, therefore, been the reason for the trouble I had encountered when comparing the observed charge with that calculated with the equation 6(1) above, and I could therefore accept my original hypothesis that this, indeed, represented the correct charge when two stones are placed together. No doubt the reader will immediately ask: 'If the church walls had been causing me to overestimate the charge in pairs of stones, what about all the single stones I had been measuring over the years?' Very true, but up to this time I had, as I mentioned above, been working in the vestry, which appears to be outside the complex field of the main church building. However, after this discovery I was careful to make all such measurements inside something like a primitive Faraday Cage, constructed of 1-inch gauge wire-netting.

We can, therefore, now consider the implications that follow from equation 6(1). Firstly, what is the effect of placing an uncharged stone alongside a charged one? Consideration of the equation indicates that it depends on their relative masses. Since one of the stones is uncharged, the term $C_2 \times M_2$ in this equation will be zero, and, if its mass is very small compared with that of the charged stone, the right-hand side of the equation becomes

$$\frac{C_1 \times M_1}{M_1}$$

which is, of course, simply the charge of the larger stone alone. This was a useful conclusion, because it meant that I was then able to measure the charge of a standing stone by hammering a small stone (e.g. of about 100g) alongside, and then measuring this with the gyrometer in the church at my leisure. It is often not very easy to balance the gyrometer on the top of a pointed standing stone in a gale!

Secondly, equation 6(1) may be written as follows:

$$C_o = \frac{(C_1 \times M_1) + (C_2 \times M_2) + \ldots\ldots (C_n \times M_n)}{M_1 + M_2 + \ldots\ldots M_n} \quad \ldots\ldots 6(2)$$

where 'n' is the total number of stones in a pile. This means that, when considering the charge on a cairn made up of many stones of differing masses and possibly different charges, the overall charge is made up of the sum of their individual powers divided by the total mass. To confirm this, one would, of course, have to dismantle the cairn and then weigh, and measure the charge on each individual stone — a not very feasible proposition. But it does mean that to measure the power of a cairn, if one can estimate the total mass, one has only to multiply this by the overall charge, e.g. by hammering a small stone alongside.

It is also of interest to consider what happens when one places a small, highly charged stone alongside a larger, uncharged one. From equation 6(1) it is clear that the large mass of the second stone is now the important factor, and that the resulting combined charge is greatly reduced. I tried out this combination, mainly to see if there would be any lasting effect on the smaller stone after it had charged the larger one. My first two attempts were unsuccessful because I chose stones for the second one that were much too large, with the result that the combined charge was too small to measure with the gyrometer, the pendulum giving a radius of less than 2cm. At the third attempt, using a small stone weighing only 72g, I got a resultant charge of 33.6, whereas that calculated from equation 6(1) was 36.7 petrons.

The interesting point was that even after these three

attempts, I could detect no reduction in the charge of the smaller stone. This is, of course, rather obvious and bears out what might be termed 'Lethbridge's principle of conservation of charge', namely, that once a stone has been given a fixed charge, it retains it for all time. Obviously, if it lost some of its charge to every stray stone that happened to come into its field, its charge would very rapidly be depleted. As I mentioned above I have a stone arrow-head which must be all of four thousand years old, but which still has a strong male charge.

I now seemed to have enough information to start working out what happens when one moves the two stones apart. I therefore set up two stones with a joint power of 9.08 lithons on the gallery of the church, where I just had room to move them as far apart as 53 feet. I then marked out stations at 0, 13, 23, 33, 43, and 53 feet, and placing a tin tray at either end of the line to screen any influence from the building. (It may well be wondered why I suddenly reverted to the use of feet here, having used metric units in most other experiments. The truth is that my steel tape is graduated in feet, and it was easier to use this and to convert my results to metres at a later stage.) The strength of the line between the two stones was measured with the gyrometer, moving one of the stones to each of these stations in turn, the other remaining stationary. This process was repeated three times, about two to three hours intervening between each series, so that different values of $\psi$ were involved. The mean strength of the line in petrons was worked out for each station and the results plotted against the distance (Figure 9). The whole procedure was then repeated, but this time with two stones having a joint power of 0.73 lithons, and the results plotted on the same graph.

It will be clearly seen from this graph that the fall in strength of the intervening line between the stones was precisely proportional to the distance separating them, and also that the **rate** of this decrease was greater with the pair of stones having the smaller power than it was with the other pair. This, therefore, had to be looked into in more detail. I also noticed that both lines on this graph passed through the zero value for separation at the calculated values rather than those measured

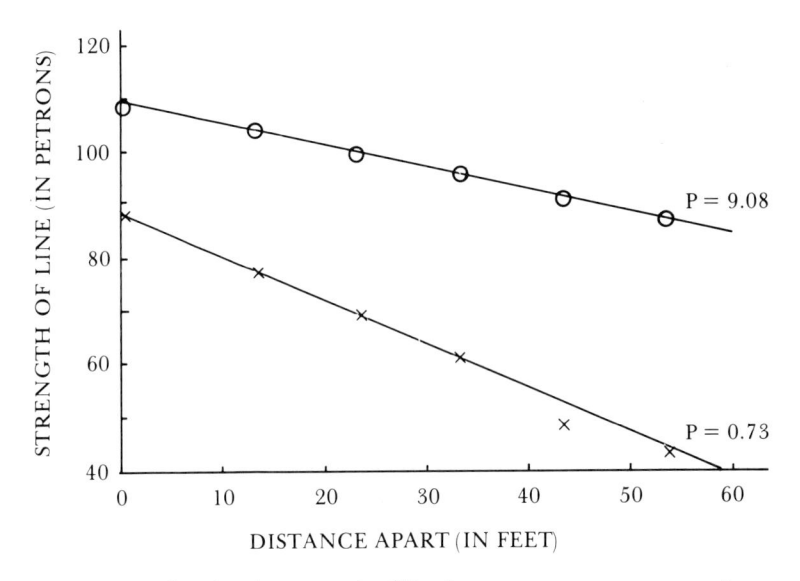

Figure 9. Reduction in strength of line between two stones at various distances.

when unscreened. I had, therefore, been right in using this figure rather than that obtained with the unscreened stones.

I next collected together nine stones of varying weight and charge and arranged them in various combinations of two, so that I had twelve pairs with joint powers ranging from 0.73 lithons with the smallest pair, to 10.75 with the greatest. Each pair was dealt with in the same manner as described above, so that I got twelve lines similar to those shown in Figure 9. From each of these lines it was then possible to work out a mean rate of decrease in strength per foot of separation for each pair of stones.

Since each pair of stones had a different joint charge at zero separation, I expressed the rate of decrease as a percentage of this figure. The results of these calculations were plotted against the power of each pair of stones (see Figure 22, Appendix B). Twelve rather scattered points are not very many to draw any very firm conclusions from, but it must be realized that to produce these twelve points entailed a very great deal of work. Thus, there were twelve pairs of stones, each at six stations, and each measurement was repeated three times — making 216 measurements with the gyrometer, together with the labour of moving the stones from one station to another between each measurement. It remained to be seen if I had done enough to get at least some idea of the correct answer.

What I really wanted was some kind of formula* by which, given the weight and charge (and thus the power) of two standing stones and the distance separating them, I would be able to calculate the strength of the line between them. Unfortunately, as I shall be showing later, such a concept is quite impractical, because such stones are not isolated from their environment, as my experimental stones in the church had been.

However, after careful consideration of the results I had obtained, I produced an equation with the various factors outlined above. The arguments by which I reached this conclusion are given in Appendix B, and the formula there given is referred to as Equation 6(3) in the text hereafter.

Does this make sense if applied to two standing stones, each weighing one tonne, with a charge of 100 petrons each? They would thus have a joint power of 2000 lithons, and if separated by a distance of 1 kilometre, the reduction in the zero separation strength of 100 would be just 9.15 per cent, given a line-strength of 90.85 petrons — which seems quite reasonable.

Two stones in line do not, however, make a classical ley line. I now had to go on to see what would happen if I added a third stone to the pairs already used. To examine this, two stones (nos 7 and 11) were set up on the church gallery 13 feet apart, giving a line between them with a strength of 112.3 petrons.

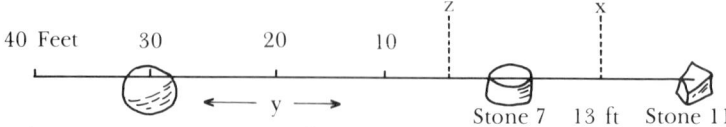

Figure 10. Arrangement of experiment with three stones in line.

*The equation 6(3) finally adopted was:

$$S_L = C_o - [C_o D \div (24.4 + 5.45 \; \Sigma \; P)]$$

Where $S_L$ is the strength of the line between the two stones, $C_o$ the joint charge of the stones when placed together, D the distance separating them in metres, and $\Sigma$ P the sum of the powers of the two stones.

# LINES AND THE CHARGE IN STONES

Five other stones, with powers ranging from 0.336 to 5.915 lithons, were then placed in turn at distances of 10, 20, 30, and 40 feet from stone No. 7, and in each case the strength of the line between stones 7 and 11 was then measured with the gyrometer (see Figure 10).

From equation 6(3) (note, p.74) it was possible to calculate what was the theoretical strength of the line between stone 7 and the various stones at these distances. I thus had a set of 20 pairs of figures for the strengths of the lines between stone 7 and the various stones, and the resulting measured line between stones 7 and 11. These results were subjected to an Analysis of Covariance, giving the 'highly significant' relation:

$$y = 63.4 + 0.563\ x \ldots \ldots 6(4)$$

where 'y' is the strength of the line between stones 7 and 11 and 'x' the calculated strength of the lines beyond stone 7, i.e. between it and the various other stones.

Now I noted that the mean value of 'y' was 112.3, which is very near to the value (111.3) of the strength of the line between stone 7 and 11 before any extra stones were added beyond stone 7, and that 'y' varied from 93.0 to 131.7 (see

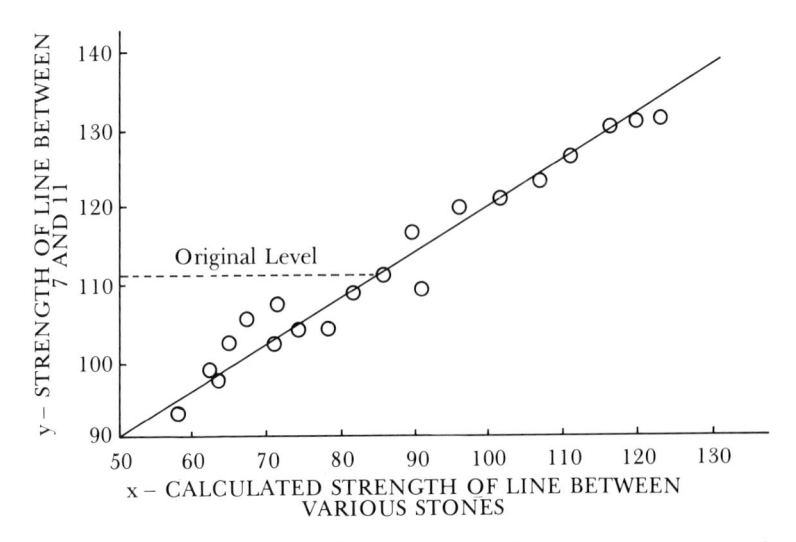

Figure 11. Strength of line between stones 7 and 11, with external line of various strengths.

Figure 11). The average calculated value of the lines beyond stone 7 was 86.8, and varied from 58.0 to 123.9. This meant that raising the external line above the figure of 86.8 had increased the strength of the line between stones 7 and 11, and that decreasing the external line below this value had similarly decreased the strength of the line between stone 7 and 11, below the figure at which it had been before any external stones had been added. This obviously complicated the situation considerably. It was no good my going out and measuring the size and charge of two standing stones, together with the distance separating them, and then hoping to calculate the strength of the intervening line with the aid of equation 6(3). These stones would inevitably have lines extending from them, in both directions, to other stones in the ley line, and these would influence the strength of the line under consideration. In fact, further investigation, as will be seen, showed that the situation was still more complicated than it had proved so far to be.

It will be remembered that the strength of the line beyond stone 7, when various stones had been placed in line and varied in distance, had been calculated by means of equation 6(3). I thought it would be a good idea if I checked these external lines, since, if the line between stones 7 and 11 could be altered by varying the external line, surely the external line could be varied by that between 7 and 11, although the distance between them was fixed throughout the experiment. I therefore reversed the whole procedure of the previous experiment and this time measured the strength of the lines between stone 7 and the stones set out at varying distances. The results gave a good straight line, which on analysis produced the equation:

$$z = 75.28 + 0.4887\ x \ldots \ldots 6(5)$$

where 'x' is the calculated strength of these lines, as in equation 6(4), and 'z' is the actual value as measured (Figure 12). This means that by adding the line between stones 7 and 11, which originally had a value of 111.3, the strength of the lines between stone 7 and the various stones used had been increased above their calculated values, but that this increase was inversely proportional to the size of the original value.

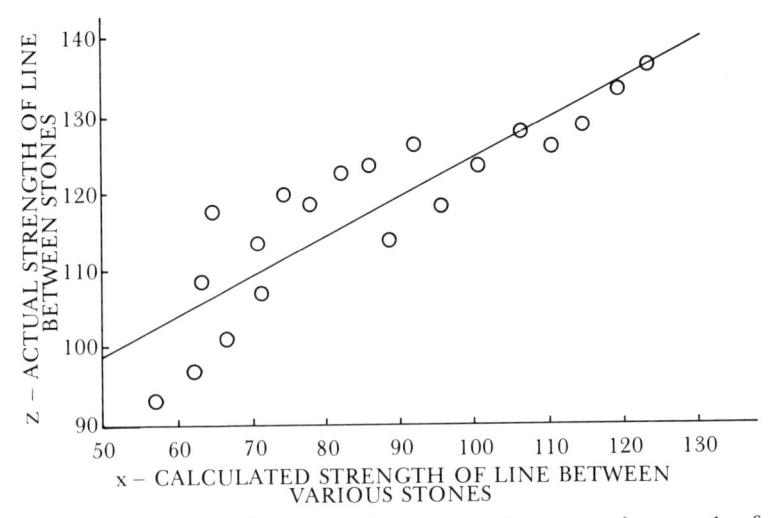

[Figure: scatter plot with x-axis "x – CALCULATED STRENGTH OF LINE BETWEEN VARIOUS STONES" from 50 to 130, and y-axis "z – ACTUAL STRENGTH OF LINE BETWEEN STONES" from 90 to 140, showing a positive linear relationship]

Figure 12. Relation between calculated and measured strength of external line.

This whole relationship, can, of course, be considered only as a 'one-off' situation, since I had used only one value (111.3) for the fixed-distance line. To investigate the complete relationship, the whole experiment should have been repeated at least a dozen times in order to get a reasonable set of figures for consideration. However, this one experiment alone had entailed making 120 individual measurements with the gyrometer, and I did not feel inclined to repeat it twelve times, especially as my next investigation showed that the situation was even more complicated than it had so far proved to be, and that any attempt to formulate an overall relationship would prove a waste of time.

Thinking how the situation, as known so far, could be applied to standing stones and ley lines in the field, I recalled that no natural standing stone had a single ley line running through it, as had my experimental stones; most of them seemed to have three, plus one which ended (or started) there. If adjoining sectors of a line had such an effect on each other, could the other two lines passing through the stone at an angle also have an effect on it? To test this, I set up two stones (Nos. 21

and 11) in line on the gallery, twenty feet apart, and **without** screens at either end, so that I had a continuous line from wall to wall. The strength of the line between these two stones was then measured, and proved to be 105.8 petrons. Two other stones were then set at 4 and 6 feet on either side of stone No. 11, so that the line between them was at right-angles to the previous line passing through stone 11. The line between stones 21 and 11 was then again measured with the gyrometer and proved to be now 123.7 petrons. Next I measured the strength of the crossing line and found this to be 127.1. I then repeated the whole procedure with two much smaller stones on the crossing line, these having a line between them with a strength of only 71.9, and found that now the line between stones 21 and 11 was only 83.8. In other words, by crossing my original line of 105.8, by another line of greater strength, I had increased its value, but when the crossing line was weaker, the original line had been reduced in strength.

Standing stones, as I pointed out in Chapter 2, usually have an odd number of ley lines i.e. one line ends (or starts) at the stone and does not run through it to form another line on the other side. Does such a truncated line have the same influence on the remaining lines as does a line passing right through, as illustrated above? To test this, I set up the same experiment with stone Nos. 21 and 11 twenty feet apart, but, instead of having two stones opposite stone 11, I had this time only one, six feet away, with a tin tray on the other side to prevent any influence there from the church walls. I then measured again the strength of the line between stones 21 and 11 and found it had been raised to 117.6 petrons, i.e. not so much as when the two stones had been opposite it, but quite an appreciable degree of increase.

A possible explanation of this apparently complex situation may be that a line arriving at a stone modifies its 'effective' charge. Thus, its power would then be altered and this would modify all the other lines running to that stone. This would be a most complex model, quite beyond my limited means to substantiate.

One other aspect had to be looked into: standing stones can have a female (negative?) charge, reacting to a pendulum with a length of 72.5cm. How would this affect my calculations? I set up two female stones, of known weight and charge, 20 feet apart and measured the strength of the line between them, but this time with a 72.5cm pendulum. This worked out at 84.6 petrons. I then calculated the theoretical strength, using equation 6(3), and this came to 84.3 petrons — a figure quite surprisingly close. This experiment was then repeated, but using a female stone at one end and a male one at the other. Measurements this time came to 96.9, with a calculated figure of 92.9. These measurements were made with both the 60cm and 72.5cm pendulums, but this made no difference when this factor was allowed for in the calculations. It was clear, therefore, that, even if the charge on two adjoining standing stones is of opposite polarity, equation 6(3) holds good for calculating the strength of the line between them.

However, my idea of being able to go out into the countryside and find two adjoining standing stones, measure their size and charge, and then with a few quick stabs at my pocket calculator, predict the strength of the line between them, was obviously no more than a pipe-dream. Such a line would be modified by the powers of all the other stones and lines in the area. Even if this could be known, any variation in one would at once affect all the others in the whole intricate complex.

In spite of all this, I decided that I really ought to check my findings in the real world, since so far I had been working with mere pebbles. I had already worked out the size and approximate weight of the Rhu-na-Bidh Stone and the Square Stone of Camus Beithe, and I knew that they were just about 750 metres apart. I now set out to measure the charge on each of these stones and the strength of the line between them. For convenience I did this by hammering small stones, each of about 100g, on these two stones. strictly speaking, the strength of the line between them should have been measured at each end at the same moment in case there was any variation in strength during the twenty minutes it took me to walk from one stone to the other. However, as there was only about 1 per cent of difference in the two values obtained at either end, it is clear that the line had not changed appreciably during this interval. For good measure, I also hammered stones on the

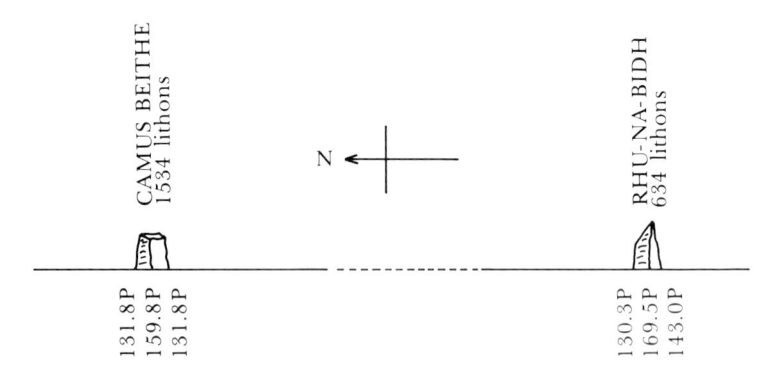

```
CAMUS BEITHE
1534 lithons                    N ←——|——→              RHU-NA-BIDH
                                                       634 lithons
```

```
     131.8P                                    130.3P
     159.8P                                    169.5P
     131.8P                                    143.0P
```

Figure 13. Strength of ley line between Rhu-na-Bidh and Camus Beithe standing stones.

lines extending beyond the two stones. The values obtained for the various strengths are shown in Figure 13, together with the charge on each stone. Since the weights of the stones were known (374 and 960 kilos), it was possible to work out what would have been the theoretical strength of the line between them, **had they been screened from outside influences.** This worked out at 152.7 petrons, a figure rather higher than the 131 obtained by measuring. But, of course, I did not know what the effect of the other lines and stones in the area might be. The line running north from the Camus Beithe Stone had just about the same value, but I do not know what the next stone in that direction might be, because it here crosses the Loch to the Diabaig side. Running south, the line was stronger; it runs to the burial cairn in the village, but there is, to my knowledge, at least one small crossing stone in between. Taking all this into consideration, it seemed that my extrapolation from pebbles to standing stones was not too wildly out.

The Rhu-na-Bidh Stone.

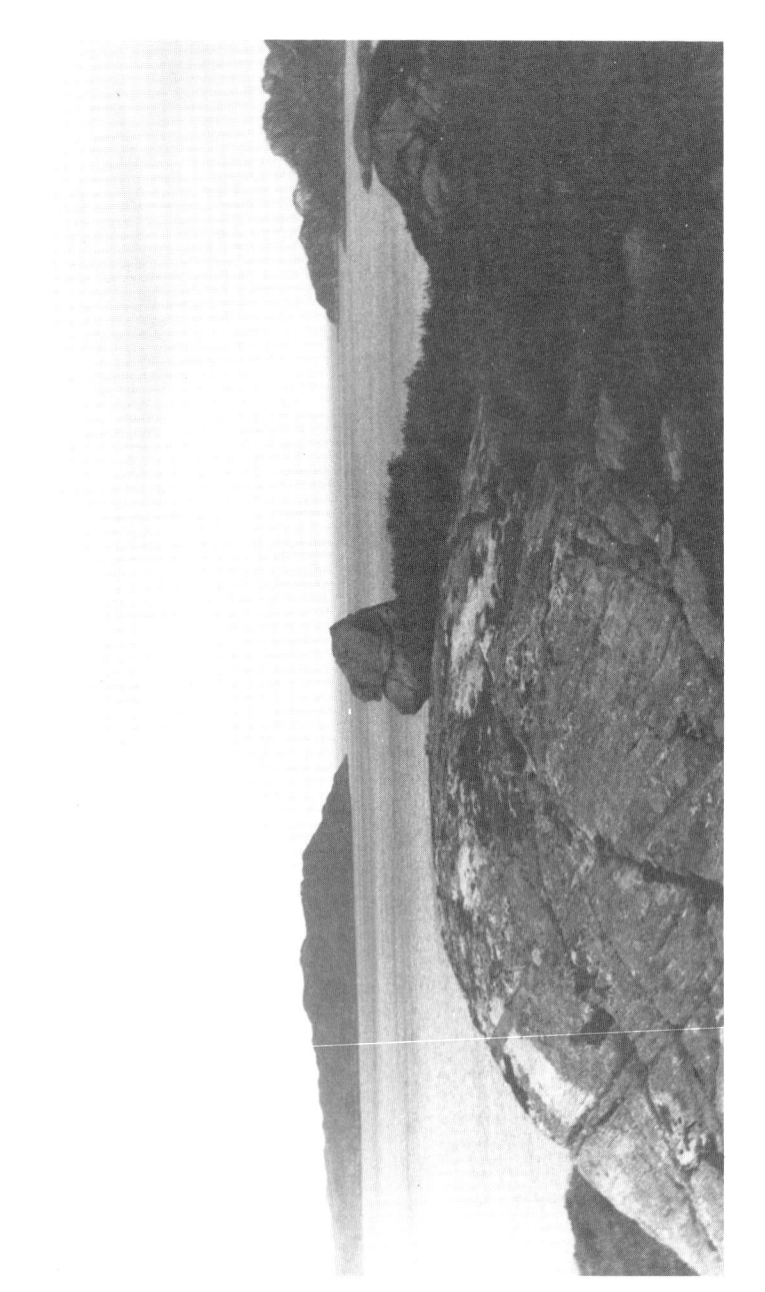

Camus Beithe Stone and the Ardislaig Gap.

The Arina Stone.

The Loch a Mhuillin Cairn.

Standing stone in the centre of Fearnmore.

Ley centre on the side of Ben Shieldaig. Stones are on the small hillock, in the centre of the photograph, showing dark against sunlit Ben Damph in the distance.

Loch-na-Beiste looking east. The ley line crosses the centre of the loch to a standing stone above the cliff to the left.

An Für standing stone overlooking Loch Shieldaig.

An Für standing stone from below.

An Faire Cairn overlooking Loch Shieldaig.

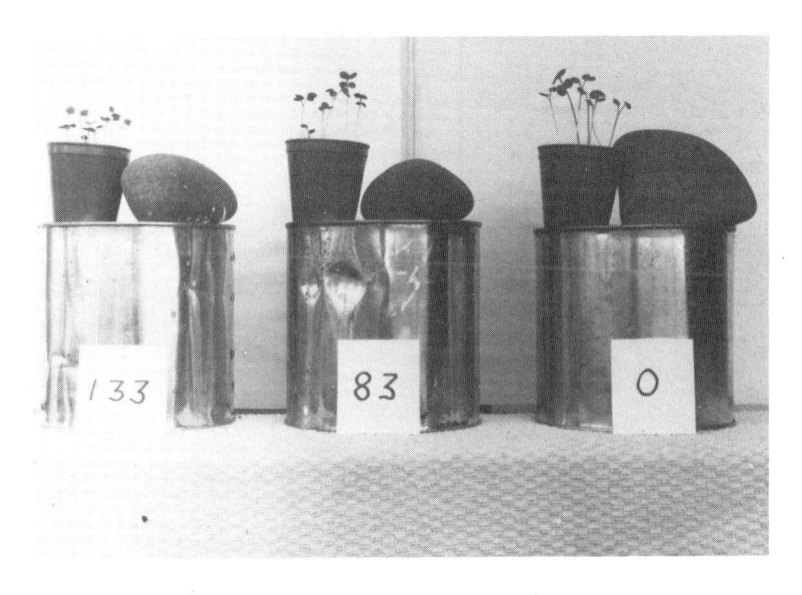

Bioassay of stone charge. The stones and pots of mustard seed are placed inside the open tins. The figures indicate the charge.

Using the portable gyrometer.

# 7.
# What are Ley Lines?

In view of what we have discussed so far, is it possible to gain some insight into how ley lines were formed and whether in fact they were man-man? There seem to be two alternative explanations; either they are a natural product of the earth's forces, or they were constructed by megalithic man for some particular purpose. We shall postpone consideration of their possible purpose to the next chapter.

There can be no doubt that the features listed by Watkins are all man-made, but can it be possible that these were all placed on some terrestial phenomena that occur in exactly straight lines? If so, what are these phenomena? Paul Screeton, in his survey of ley line knowledge[21] suggests that, as the earth cooled an intricate grid of geodetic lines was formed, possibly magnetic or gravitational in character. Tom Graves[12] suggests that megalithic man was aware of this and placed his 'needles of stone' over the crossing points of these lines in order to bring these forces to the surface for some specific and unknown purpose. There is, however, no direct evidence that these underground geodetic lines ran in straight lines. Indeed, the whole of Underwood's work[26] suggests that they wander about in a most intricate pattern of curves; it is only the 'overgrounds', or ley lines, that run for long distances in straight lines.

The work that I have described in previous chapters has suggested that something indistinguishable from ley lines can be detected running between two charged stones. Is it possible that megalithic man realized this and set up his ley lines by charging stones and other objects in a straight line, so that the energy flowing between two stones carried on to others in the same line? If this is true, it must be shown that there is a greater flow of energy when the line is straight than when it is not so aligned. To investigate that I set up two stones (Nos. 12 and 21) of fairly high power on the church gallery, screened at each end. A third stone (No. 7), of lesser power, was then placed 20 feet from stone 21, but 3 feet from the line extended from that between stones 12 and 21. As will be seen from Figure 14, this just allowed the parallels of the line between stones 7 and 21 to overlap those on the original line extended from stone 12 and 21. The strength of the line between stones 7 and 21 was then measured and this proved to be 148.8 petrons. Stone 7 was then moved 4½ feet from the centre of the direct line between stones 12 and 21, and the strength again measured. Care had to be taken that the gyrometer was still within the parallels of the line from 21 and 7, i.e. some 8 feet from stone 21; beyond this point there was no detectable line owing to the screen at the end of the gallery. The strength of the side line was now only 111.5 petrons; a reduction of just over 25 per cent due to the three stones not being in a straight line.

My conclusions from all this were that, if three stones lie sufficiently near to a straight line so that their parallels overlap, conditions as outlined in equations 6(4) and (5) become effective and energy is passed from one sector of the line to another. If, however, the parallels do not overlap, the separate

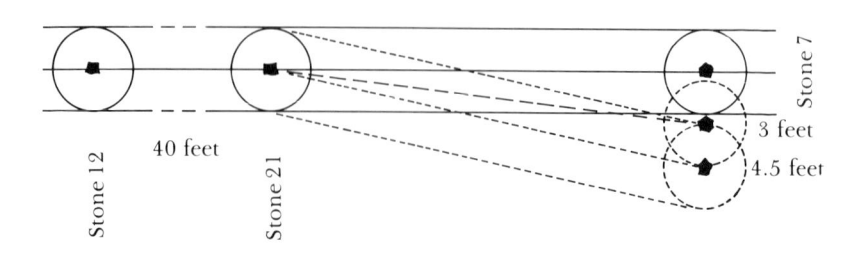

Figure 14. Effect of moving a stone 3 feet and 4½ feet out of line with two other stones.

## WHAT ARE LEY LINES?

sections of line are similar to separate ley lines running through these stones and have less direct effect on one another. There is, therefore, a very distinct gain in the strength of a line if its various sections are approximately in a straight line.

Just how approximate can this be? It is obvious that, the further apart the stones are, the closer to a straight line they have to be in if their parallels are to overlap. Indeed, it is possible to calculate that, if three stones, each almost zero in dimension, are 1km apart, they may not depart from the straight by more than 0.08 seconds of arc. Obviously, standing stones are always larger than this, and if, say, they were 1 metre in diameter, the divergence could then be 0.14 seconds of arc.

If this rule of straightness is so strict, what about stone circles, where many observers have noted the flow of energy round their stones? The constructors of Stonehenge may well have known about this situation and overcome it by connecting their standing stones by a series of lintels, thus connecting adjoining stones and in effect making the whole structure into a single stone. On the other hand, the stones of a stone circle can be so close that they are almost touching, and there would then be a large overlap of their parallels. If there are sufficient stones making up a circle their parallels may still overlap sufficiently and a free flow of energy will pass round the circle. The Thoms[23] give a list (their Table 311) of some eleven circles that they believe were still relatively complete, together with their diameter and number of stones. These circles varied from 20.9 to 106.2 feet in diameter, with a mean of 68.4 feet. From the data I gave above, it is possible to calculate the minimum number of stones making a circle of given diameter so that their parallels will always overlap. Assuming that the stones averaged 1 metre in diameter, some 12.9 stones would be required for a circle 68.4 feet in diameter. In actual fact the mean number of stones in the Thoms' table is 13.5. However, on inspection of their data, three of the eleven sites would not have had sufficient stones, with one other site a marginal case, if the stones were only 1 metre in diameter.

Can we assume, therefore, that megalithic man could have set up his grid of ley lines simply by charging stones or other objects, as I have described in previous chapters, and placing them in straight lines or circles? On the face of it this would appear possible, but on considering this idea I found one major difficulty.

I have described in earlier chapters that there is an important ley centre and standing stone (Rhu-na-Bidh) close to my church and that this latter is built of dressed stone, which must have received some charge from the masons cutting the stones used to build it. On surveying the Rhu-na-Bidh Stone I had, however, noted no lines towards the relatively recently built church, whereas if the above theory is correct, there surely should have been. I thought I had better make sure of this; so I walked up and down the side of the church nearest the standing stone with the Oasis Rod in my hand. After much searching I was just able to detect two weak lines running from the stone towards those parts of the church where I had noted the two blind springs as described in Chapter 2. I carefully located the centres of both these lines and hammered a small stone on each. On measuring the charge on these two stones with the gyrometer, I found they were 53.6 and 52.5 petrons, and on measuring the distance between the standing stone and the two blind springs, I found figures of 78.7 and 87.5 metres respectively.

Now I have repeatedly mentioned using the line between these two blind springs in the church to charge stones, and the strength of this line averages about 118 petrons. The combined mass of the dressed stones making up the church must be very considerable, and, if this was their overall charge, these two lines running from the Rhu-na-Bidh Stone should be far stronger than the above figures suggest. There is also the difficulty, which I have mentioned before, that on throwing stones at the church wall I could obtain no indication of charge on the outside of the walls. What, then, was wrong with my theory that ley lines always run between two charged objects?

It will be recalled that, when I was describing my early work in the Church, I had been unable to locate any geodetic lines such as Underwood described, under this building, and I had assumed that the modern architects had been unaware that a sacred edifice should be sited so that it lies over a suitable pattern of such lines. I had also found two blind springs in the church at either end of the central line; but, from what Underwood had said, this pattern may be no more than a phenomenon that forms at either end of a geodetic line of any kind. I had also found blind springs at most, if not all, ley centres, and since all such centres have an odd number of ley lines running to them, one of these lines must terminate and form a blind spring. Also mark stones, where two lines cross, do not show any indication of blind springs or crossed streams.

What else was my church lacking which is present at a ley centre and which attracts lines? The answer might be crossed streams, but as will be seen later there may be another explanation. But if this is the reason for the low strength of the lines to the church, it follows that there must be sufficient stream crossings in an area for the megalithic designer to have found one in just the right place to set up his ley centre. Is this very likely?

Although I have ranged up and down the north of the Applecross peninsula and around Shieldaig in my ley hunting, I have found no area with more lines per square kilometre than around Doire-aona (Figure 15) and the Shieldaig peninsula (Figure 16). In the former area, comprising 8.7 square kilometres, I have found 20 ley centres and 47 lines, averaging 1.2km between centres. In the latter area, comprising only 3.1 square kilometres, I have found 20 centres and 35 lines, averaging 0.83km between centres.

Now around Shieldaig and the northern part of Doire-aona district the underlying rock is Lewisian Gneiss, which is immensely contorted, being very ancient, and full of faults, as shown by the geological maps. To the south of Doire-aona the rock is Torridonian Sandstone, with very few faults. Through these faults in the Lewisian Gneiss water drains, so there are few surface streams and in consequence there will be frequent opportunities for crossed streams to occur below ground. Perhaps, therefore, the great number of ley centres on the Lewisian Gneiss may be accounted for in this way. This is, indeed, supported by the fact that ten of the twenty centres around Doire-aona occur in the 2 square kilometres overlying the Lewisian, while the other ten are in the 6.7 square kilometres on Torridonian. Lewisian Gneiss also occurs on the

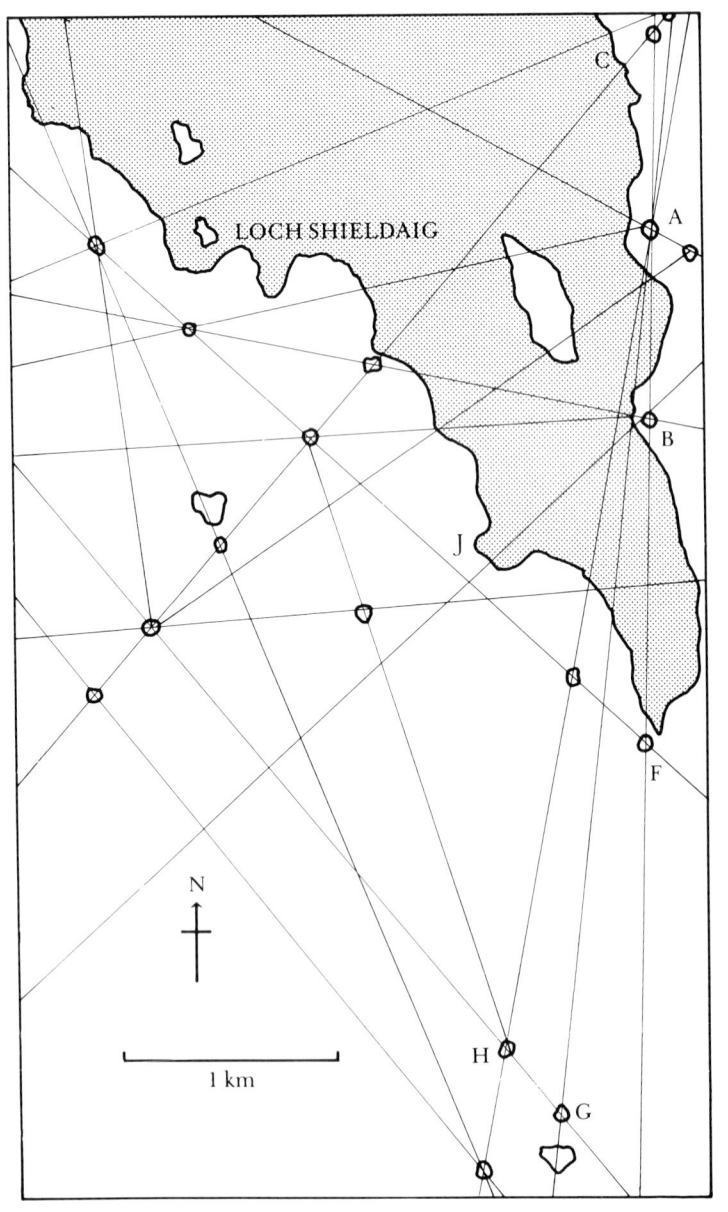

A. Rhu-na-Bidh.  B. Burial cairn.  C. Camus Beithe.  G. An Für.  H. An Faire.
J. Doire-aona.

Figure 15. Ley lines discovered around Doire-aona.

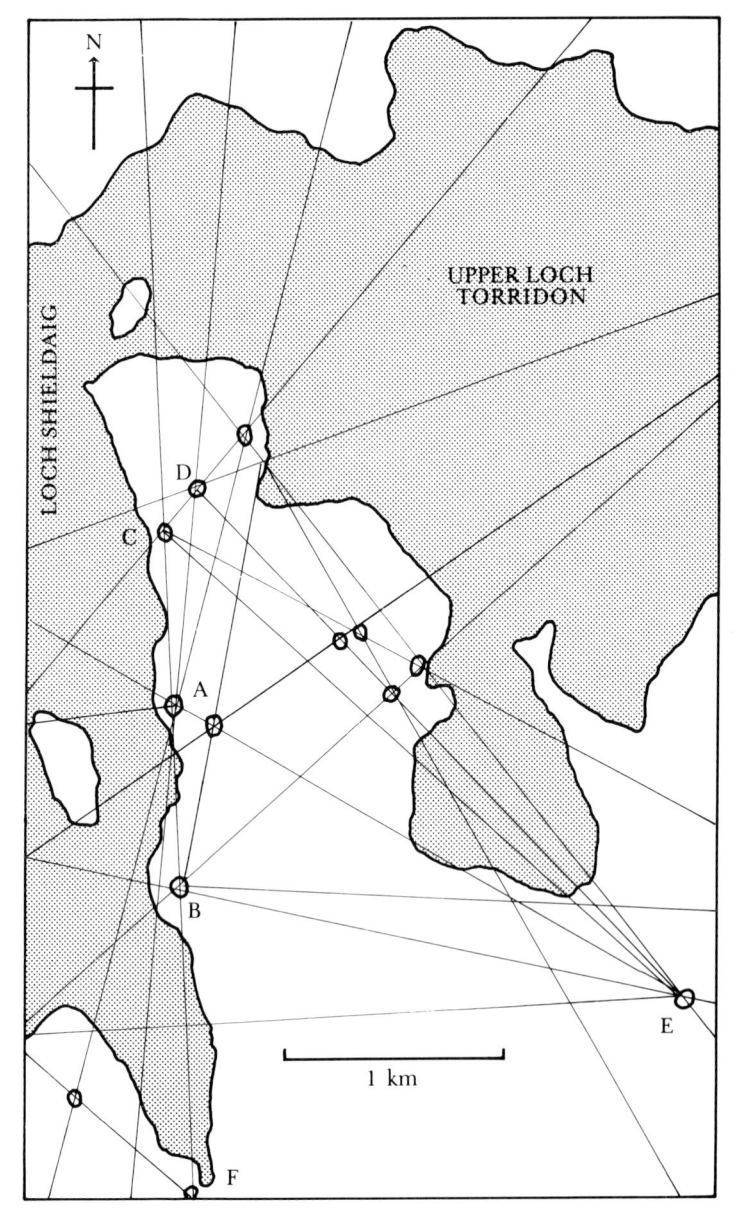

A. Rhu-na-Bidh.  B. Burial cairn.  C. Camus Beithe.  D. Cnoc Ruadh.  E. Hill at side of Ben Shieldaig.  F. Flint factory.

Figure 16. Ley lines discovered on Shieldaig peninsula.

Diabaig side of the Loch, and from the little work I have been able to do in that area it would appear that there are many centres to be found there also.

Any reasonable theory that is not just idle speculation should be amenable to checking in the field. It is not, of course, possible to prove that all ley centres are sited over crossed streams, but, if many observations are made and no such centre is found without its accompanying streams, the probability that the theory is correct becomes great. On the other hand, if after careful searching no such streams are found below just one centre, the theory is disproved. So far, after examining over sixty sites, I have not found one where there is not some indication of two crossing streams running below.

Another test would be to examine an area where ley lines are frequent — such as the two I have mentioned — and plot **all** the crossing points of underground streams, as well as fault lines, since 'dry' streams seem to be equally effective. Inspection of the resulting chart would indicate whether or not the number of sites is sufficient to have allowed megalithic man to find points in straight lines on which to place his ley centres. Unfortunately, I am not sufficiently proficient as a water diviner to undertake such a task.

Even if it is found that there are sufficient crossed geodetic lines for this purpose, there are, I think, two further objections to the theory that this grid is based on a natural phenomenon. Firstly, the form of the charge observed on standing stones (either the male or female rate) is found to be **inherent** only in living (or once living) material. Secondly, one would expect to find sites unused by the ley complex where this charge is present in the ground. So far I have found no evidence of this.

Looking back at what we have been able to discover about the properties of ley lines, is it possible to make some sort of a guess as to their physical nature? Firstly, I think it must be accepted that they are some form of energy; otherwise the dowser would surely not be able to react to them. Many writers have suggested that this energy is electromagnetic in form. Certainly many of the properties of ley lines, as described in earlier chapters, bear a close similarity to those of electricity and magnetism — so much so that I have been at pains to

## WHAT ARE LEY LINES?

suggest terms different from those used in electricity in order to avoid confusion. There are, however, some fundamental differences. For example, the rate of decrease in strength of a line as two stones are moved apart does not conform to the inverse square law; also, as shown above, the charge of one stone is not diminished when charging another, so this force does not appear to conform to the law of conservation of energy.*

This ley energy seems to fit most closely with the mysterious Odic force described by Baron Karl von Reichenbach[19], who said its properties lay somewhere between magnetism and light — both of course, forms of electromagnetic energy. One interesting point he made was that this force could be reflected by an ordinary glass mirror. I tried this out with both my lines between two charged stones and also with the ley lines running from the Rhu-na-Bidh stone, and found that it was indeed the case. This led me to the idea that it might be possible to estimate the wavelength of these lines by the well-known interference method. I will not weary the reader, unfamiliar with this method with a long and confusing explanation; suffice it to say that if a ray travelling out from an object is reflected directly back on itself by means of a mirror or other reflecting surface, the two rays travelling in opposite directions interfere with each other. On examination of the combined ray, one finds bands of high amplitude alternating with areas where the two rays cancel each other out. The distance between two such peaks (or two troughs) is equal to half the wavelength (see Figure 17).

Two male-charged stones were laid 20 feet apart on the church gallery, with screens at either end, so that there was a line between them but none beyond them. A mirror was then

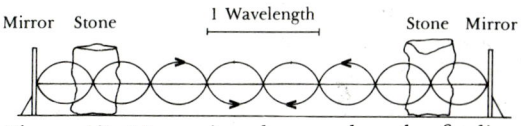

Figure 17. Measuring the wavelength of a line.

* On the other hand, as the famous Einstein equation $E = MC^2$ shows, energy is equivalent to mass. Thus the exchange of charge between stones may result in a loss of mass rather than energy. Since C (the velocity of light) is extremely large, the loss in mass would be too minute to detect.

set up 20 feet from one of the stones and carefully aligned so that the stones and their reflections appeared to be in line. The area between the mirror and the nearest stone was then examined with the pendulum, and I found that there was now a line here where there had been none before but that it consisted of bands of strong reaction, alternating with a nil reaction when the pendulum oscillated instead of gyrating. I found it easier to estimate the position of the nil reaction than those of maximum gyration, and marked off six of these positions on the floor. Measuring the distance between these marks in centimetres gave me a mean half-wavelength of $58.0 \pm 0.67$, the full wavelength of course being double this figure. I then repeated this procedure with two female-charged stones and obtained a half-wavelength of $70.0 \pm 0.55$ cm. From this it would appear that the male and female charges are merely different wavelengths of the same force and not of different polarity, as has sometimes been thought. This is supported by the fact that a stone can be charged with both the male and female rate at one and the same time.

Later I measured the wavelength of the central line in the church, which also reacted to the male rate. This turned out to be rather confusing, because I found two sets of nil points, one giving a half-wavelength of $72.6 \pm 1.31$ cm, and another at $31.4 \pm 0.41$ cm. There must apparently be some other rate running down this line that I have not so far been able to identify.

I next tried out this technique on one of the lines running north from the Rhu-na-Bidh Stone. This reacted to the male rate with the pendulum, but gave me a mean half-wavelength of $97.2 \pm 0.41$ cm. There were, therefore, several different wavelength values associated with the male reaction to the pendulum, and so there seems to be no evidence that the rate is a measure of the 'rate of vibrations' of this property, as many writers have suggested, unless, of course the velocity of travel of the energy is also varying. At present I can see no simple method of measuring this velocity, and this must await more sophisticated instrumentation than the simple pendulum.

If these wavelengths are electromagnetic in form, and therefore travel at the speed of light, their frequency range would lie between 470 and 150 MHz, being slightly shorter in wavelength than the ultra-short-wave used by Herz in his early experiments and the micro-waves used by Oliver Lodge. It is of interest to note that both these radio waves can be reflected in a suitable mirror. If, indeed, ley line energy is of this form, there seems to be no good reason why it should not be picked up by a suitably designed radio set, but such expertise is well outside my range of knowledge.

This property of ley lines to be reflected suggests an interesting idea. Examining the Thoms' figure (11,5) outlining their idea of the geometry of Stonehenge, I noticed that the inner trilithons are thought to lie on an elipse, open at the north end to form a U. If a ley line was shot into one limb of the U, it would travel round to emerge from the other limb and then cross the original line at some distant point, causing interference phenomena. If another U was sited on the opposite side of this point, this line would then return, again causing interference and a massive standing wave at the point of intersection. In fact, this could form something very like an early (primitive?) laser. There would, of course, be no line there now, because the trilithons are in a sad state of ruin, but a careful search of the ground might show some signs of the original structures and form the purpose of a fine ley hunt.

It occurred to me that I might be able to use this laser effect to raise the charge in stones to a much higher level than I had hitherto obtained. Starting with four stones hammered in my hand, all gave a charge of 108.7 petrons. Two were set out about 14 feet apart on the church gallery, with a mirror at each end just beyond each stone. Using the pendulum, I carefully adjusted the two stones so that the distance between them was, as near as I could judge, equal to five wavelengths and each mirror one-half wavelength beyond its stone. I now had a series of peaks and troughs of line strength between these two stones, the amplitude of the peaks being theoretically twice the strength of the original line. The two other male stones were then placed as near a peak as possible, hammered, and the charge measured with the gyrometer. These two stones, which now had an augmented charge, were then substituted for the two in front of the mirrors and the whole process repeated.

This was then repeated over a dozen times, the charge finally being raised to a figure of 180 petrons. Theoretically, the charge should have been doubled each time this process was repeated, but in actual fact the increment in charge only averaged 14.5 petrons, and as the process was repeated, this became smaller and smaller. This small increment was probably due to the difficulty of measuring the wavelength with any great degree of accuracy and also of locating the exact position of the peak.

The whole experiment was repeated, but this time using four female-charged stones with a starting charge of about 85 petrons. This time, after repeating the process over a dozen times, I was able to reach a figure of 183.3 petrons. It does look, therefore, as if there may be a maximum charge, which is more and more difficult to attain as one approaches it; but it would appear that, by using suitable techniques, it is possible artificially to raise the induced charge in stones to a figure nearly double that of the inherent level.

# 8.
# The Purpose of Ley Lines

If ley lines were really made by megalithic man and were not some form of natural phenomenon, it must be assumed that he had some impressive reasons for doing all this work. We can only guess as to this purpose and be guided by what we now know of the present properties of these lines and stones.

Writers on the ley phenomenon have made many such guesses. Watkin's theory that they were tracks has already been discussed, and it has been shown that this can be only partly true and was probably a secondary development. Other writers, as described by Paul Screeton[21], have suggested that these lines were laid down as navigation tracks for UFOs. I am not in a position to make any firm judgement on this, since I cannot claim ever to have seen one of these objects. However, a few years ago one was said to have been seen locally travelling above one of the ley lines from the north, making a characteristic right-angle turn over the North Applecross coast, and then passing down the ley line I described in Chapter 3, which runs along the crest of the hills south of Loch Shieldaig. Even if this were true, such tracks could not explain the close network of lines that I have described in this work.

Sig Lonegren suggests in a recent number of *The Ley Hunter*[16] that there are really three different phenomena we are calling leys. There is the classical alignment of sites, for which he suggests the term 'T leys' or topographical leys; the straight beams of energy he calls 'E leys'; and finally the archaeoastronomical alignments that could be termed 'A leys'. These three can be concurrent or separate.

It is clear that what I have been dealing with are, presumably, E leys, since I have identified them by dowsing. However, the line I described in Chapter 3, running from the Rhu-na-Bidh Stone to Meall Mor at Fearnmore, is of all three types. As shown, it lies on the 'Beltane' line of the setting sun on 1 May, is one of a straight alignment of at least five sites, and quite definitely shows a flow of energy along it. On the other hand, the short lines just connecting adjoining sites cannot possibly be considered as classical ley lines as described by Watkins, although the energy flow along them differs in no way from that on longer alignments.

Many writers have suggested that ley energy might have been collected and used to encourage fertility of crops and domestic animals. Underwood[26] noted that mistletoe, crow garlic *(Allium vinealis)*, and various trees such as yew, hawthorn hazel, and apple, were all apparently affected by geodetic lines, often showing twisted growth when growing over blind springs, etc. I thought, therefore, that it might be interesting to see if my charged stones had any effect on plant germination and growth.

This test was set up in the same way as a regular 'agricultural' field trial. Three stones, each weighing about 1½ kilos, were collected from the beach; the first was hammered on the central male line in the church, and the second on the female side line; the third stone I was very careful not to handle at any time. Each stone was placed in an empty 7 lb jam tin so that it would be shielded from any outside influence. On each stone was placed a 2-inch plastic flowerpot, containing Levington Seed Compost. Each pot was sown with seven mustard seeds, and the three tins were placed in my sun-room to await developments. After twelve days the seedlings were large enough to weigh; so they were carefully removed from the compost, washed and dried, and the produce of each pot was weighed to the nearest 10 milligrams.

Germination was somewhat uneven; so I divided the total weight by the number of seedlings, thus obtaining the mean weight of the seedlings in each pot. The reader can imagine my surprise when I found that the seedlings grown over the male stone weighed only 56 per cent of those grown on the uncharged stone, while those grown on the female stone were 69 per cent. I at once thought that this must be due to pure chance; so I repeated the trial twice more and obtained very similar results. I was still not satisfied, since the differences might be due to some peculiarity of the uncharged stone or the tin it was in. I therefore changed the tins for three new ones and obtained three new stones from the beach. I again repeated the trial, but with the same results. The differences could not have been due to treatment, because each pot received the same quantity of water and the positions were moved round each day.

I thus had four replicates of the three treatments, i.e. male, female, and uncharged stone; so I could apply an Analysis of Variance to my results. this showed that the mean reduction in weight of the seedlings grown on the male-charged stones was 27.5 per cent less than those on the uncharged stones, while those grown on the female stones were 31.5 per cent less. There did not appear to be any significant difference in the germination between the three treatments as they averaged just over six seedlings per pot in each batch. The Analysis showed that the seedlings grown on the charged stones differed in weight significantly from those grown over the uncharged stones at a probability level of 0.05.

My next step was to see if an increasing charge caused an increase in damage to the mustard seedlings. This time four pots were set up with stones of various charges from 0 to 167 petrons. Mustard seedlings were grown in the same way and were weighed after eleven days' growth. The mean seedling weights were then plotted against the charge of the stone they were grown on (Figure 18); this showed that the weight of the seedling was inversely proportional to the charge of the stone. However, this did not prove that the cause of this decrease was the charge, since it might have been due to the power of the stone, i.e. the product of the charge multiplied by the weight. To test this I charged four stones together, so that the charge was the same in each, although their weights varied from about 200g to 1.6kg. Seedling weights, when they had grown on these stones, showed very little difference, thus proving that the factor concerned was the charge on the stones and not the power.

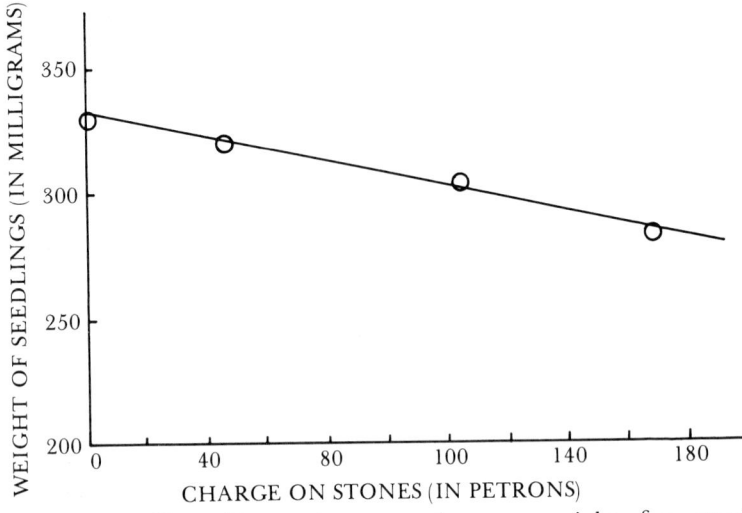

Figure 18. Effect of increasing stone charge on weight of mustard seedlings.

If a charge on stones could have such a marked effect on mustard seedlings, was this also true of the lines between them? Unfortunately, I could see no easy way of setting up a fully replicated trial to test this because all the charged stones would interact with one another and a line-free control area would only be obtainable by screening all round and this might affect yield. However, after some thought I decided to replicate in time, setting up three consecutive experiments. Each experiment consisted of two pots, each sown with the standard seven mustard seeds. One of these pots was sited half-way between two charged stones 2½ metres apart, giving a line between them with a strength of 167.5 petrons, admittedly a fairly high value; the other pot was set about a metre to one side of this line. Half way between these two pots I placed a long strip of galvanized iron, carefully arranged so that it covered the lines between both stones and the second pot. Thus one pot was on the line, but outside the circular fields of the two stones, while the other pot was fully screened from the effects of either stone. Since the screen was half way between the two pots, any environmental influence it might have was the same for both pots.

The pots were left for about ten days for the seedlings to grow; they were then harvested and weighed as in previous experiments. The whole experiment was then repeated twice more, but each time the position of the pot on the line and control pot were interchanged, or the experiment moved to an entirely different area.

The results showed that the line had much the same effect as did the charged stones; the mean weight of the seedlings was reduced by some 20.3 per cent. There was, however, one new factor: germination was markedly reduced in the pot situated on the line when compared with the screened pots, the mean reduction being as large as 52.9 per cent, a highly significant result. It was quite clear from this that both charged stones and the lines between them had a very marked effect on the growth of mustard seedlings. Moreover, this last experiment provided objective evidence that such lines must exist, the evidence provided being totally free from any taint of such 'occult' methods as dowsing.

I find it extremely difficult to think of any good reason to account for this action on mustard seedlings. Germination of seeds generally takes place when they come into contact with water in the presence of oxygen (if the oxygen is removed from the air, seeds will not germinate in the remaining nitrogen). Enzyme action is then started and germination takes place. Nothing else, other than warmth, is required, as is demonstrated by the germination of seedlings on damp blotting-paper. It is most difficult to conceive that the 'rays' from these charged stones could possibly alter these simple conditions and inhibit germination, although in a most sophisticated experiment Sister Justa Smith[22] found that the emanations from a healer's hands did in fact increase enzyme action. Certainly, atomic radiation of various wave lengths can destroy the life in dormant seeds, probably by damaging the enzymes; but surely the radiation from these stones cannot be of such power. The conditions for growth are far more sensitive to the correct environment than are those for germination, and many things can go wrong to inhibit maximum increase in size.

Finally, I tried various other types of seedling, including cress, peas, beans, and turnips. Of these, only turnips showed a response similar to that of mustard seeds. This is of interest since both mustard and turnips belong to the same botanical family, the Cruciferae. I have been asked many times why I chose mustard in the first instance and the number seven for the quantity of seedlings, both being known to be of occult significance, as John Michell showed[17]. I was not unaware of this at the time, but it so happened that I had plenty of mustard seed which had a good germination figure, and that seven seeds fit well into a two-inch pot — one in the centre, and six round it. It certainly seems strange that I should have chosen for my first test a species which gave such a good reaction. Had I chosen cress rather than mustard, I would almost certainly have carried this investigation no further.*

It was not until I had completed these experiments that I thought of testing the charge on the mustard seed, which I found to be male; but much more significantly I found that mustard seed is an interrupter. When the seed was placed alongside a male stone the pendulum refused to gyrate; when placed beside a female stone the gyrations were reversed. Turnip seed, which was the only other species to react to charged stones, behaves as an interrupter in a similar manner. Does all this mean that the seedlings of these two species are absorbing the energy radiated by the charged stones, and in doing so are in some way damaging their potential for growth?

Many ley hunters have been surprised to note groups of Caledonian Pine *(Pinus sylvestris)* growing on the tops of hills and apparently forming a feature of classic ley lines, whereas these trees could not have been growing in this position in the time of megalithic man. All living material has either a male or female charge and could, therefore, attract ley energy; but this species of pine, which gives a female reaction to the

---

*I should point out that the above technique using mustard seedlings is certainly not original in principal. It is frequently employed in both biology and medicine to assess the action of an agent when the process of that action is apparent but not understood. It is termed Bioassay. One example is the assessment of the strength of a drug, by measuring its effect on colonies of bacteria, etc. In my own branch of science, insecticides are commonly assayed by measuring the quantity required to kill 50 per cent of a batch of insects, the results being quoted as its LD50.

pendulum, is, I found, a powerful interrupter and must therefore absorb this form of energy. Why, therefore, are these trees found growing on ley lines?

Elm *(Ulmus spp.)*, as mentioned by Lethbridge, is also an interrupter, and this leads to an intriguing speculation. During the last decade or so elm trees have suffered a tragic decline in the south of England. The primary cause of this is, of course, Dutch Elm Disease and its Scolytid Bark Beetle vector. The sudden increase of this disease has been attributed by experts to a strengthening of vigour in the disease. Might it, however, be that about this time there was also a great increase in the building of motorways in this area, with the resultant fracturing of many ley lines? If these lines changed their position at that time, they might well have affected the vigour of the elm trees growing in positions previously free from this deleterious energy.

I have described these experiments in some detail for a number of reasons. Firstly, I think that it is an important illustration of the influence this form of energy, locked in the stones, has on something other than the dowser. In fact, these experiments could be carried out entirely without any skill in this art, and I think it is important that they should be repeated by other investigators with seedlings of a much larger range of species, in order that some clue can be obtained of the range of effect and possibly of the reasons for it. This will probably entail an investigation of the whole question of interrupters. Secondly, it would be perfectly possible to measure the size of the charge on a stone simply by weighing the mustard seedlings grown on it. As a technique for obtaining such a measurement it is, however, rather impracticable, since it takes about ten to fourteen days for the seedlings to grow sufficiently large to be weighed accurately, as compared with a few minutes' work with the pendulum.

Thirdly, it would seem to indicate that ley energy is not always beneficial and in laying down the system megalithic man may have been trying to rid the area of an undesirable form of energy — hence the great number of nodes in cultivated and fertile areas. The ancient Chinese geomancers were apparently well aware of this dangerous aspect, as described by Eitel,[7] and were horrified when ignorant

Europeans built their houses on a 'Dragon Line'. This idea might also lead to a re-interpretation of the dream I described in Chapter 5. Is it possible that the people I saw surrounding the stone were trying to 'degauss' the stone of its undesirable energy? The fact that they appeared to be passing something round in an anti-clockwise (widdershins) direction might well support this.

# 9.
# Interrupting Ley Lines

I had discovered how to make a ley line, but as yet I had no means of destroying one. At times I felt rather like the sorcerer's apprentice in that I had set flowing a flood of lines and did not know the spell to stop this flood. In fact, at one time the church became so full of lines from the charged stones I had stored there that I was in grave danger of having to abandon its use for further investigations.

Dowsing literature is full of recipes for the stopping of what are termed 'black streams', considered to be geodetic lines that have a detrimental effect on the health of anyone unfortunate enough to live within their influence, particularly if one's bed is sited over one of them. From what I have said about the effect of ley lines on mustard seed, etc., it is clear that they may well have a similar effect on human health as black streams. It has been pointed out that the activities of modern 'civilized' man are fracturing many existing ley lines. One only has to think of the effect of cutting a wide band across country for a modern motorway to realize what damage to the ley system must be constantly taking place. I have already described the habit of ley lines to latch on to any suitable object when 'running wild'. Should the suitable object in line be someone's dwelling, there is obvious danger that the inhabitant may suffer ill-health.

The recipes for 'stopping' black streams are many and wonderful; such practices as driving an iron stake into the ground over the black stream are said to be effective. Other dowsers have used copper wire to almost surround the building to be protected — an idea somewhat reminiscent of the wartime degaussing of ships by surrounding them with a charged copper cable to prevent them from setting off magnetic mines. Various forms of copper coil have also been used. In view of all this, I thought a few careful experiments on my lines between stones and also on ley lines might prove useful.

In Chapter 6 I have described how sheet-iron or wire-netting of a mesh smaller than 35mm could prove an effective screen for the lines I had set up between charged stones. I investigated this further by setting up two strips of iron-sheet, each 65mm in width, on a line between two stones. The gap between the two strips was gradually closed until the line vanished; at this point the width of the gap between the strips proved to be 35mm for a male line and 50mm for a female line. Whether this difference is connected with the difference in wavelength described earlier, I am not at all sure. I also found that, if the gap between the two strips was moved away from the central line, the line vanished, and that, if a strip 35mm (50mm for female) wide was placed in the direct centre of the line, it was again broken. In fact it would appear that a disc of iron, with a diameter of 35 mm for male and 50 mm for the female line, is placed exactly in the centre of the line, it will be broken. My conclusion was that, if a line was to be broken with an iron stake, it would have to be at least 50mm in width and placed on the exact centre of the line if it was to be effective. My few experiments with copper wire in the form of various coils showed that it could effectively stop a line as long as the end of the wire was held in the hand, thus presumably being charged. As soon as I let go of the wire, the line came back to life.

Recently dowsers have turned to treating the source of the line, i.e. the stone or other object concerned. The generally accepted method of doing this is to place a few chips of amethyst on the stone, this being considered enough to 'kill' it. Using some amethyst chips given to me by a stone-polishing friend, I placed three stones, A, B, and C, in line and measured the strength of the line between stones B and C. I then placed the amethyst chips on stone B and found that the strength of the line had been reduced from 117.0 to 63.8 petrons. I then removed stone B and measured the strength of the line between stones A and C, finding it to be the same, i.e. 63.8. This proved that I had 'killed' stone B with the chips, but not the line, which continued straight through it as if it had not been there. I do not feel that the expression 'killing a stone' is very apt, because the chips do not in fact completely remove the charge in the stone; it is still there after the chips are removed. I feel that 'masking' a charge is a more appropriate term.

If amethyst chips would do this, what other materials are effective? Going through my small collection of geological specimens, I tried these and other materials, such as various metals, to see if they too had this power. I soon found that, besides amethyst, quartz crystals, jasper, and flint all gave a good masking effect, while dolerite, serpentine, pegmatite and quartzite all gave some masking but were less effective than the rocks with larger quartz crystals. Lewisian Gneiss, Torridonian Sandstone and glass had no effect, nor did the metals lead and iron, which, as we have seen, can stop a line. No other metals or minerals I tried gave any masking effect. It rather looks, therefore, as if the active materials are those rocks that have relatively large quartz crystals in their make-up. The fact that glass appears to be quite inactive is interesting. The chemical constituent of quartz is silicon dioxide, while glass is made up of various mixtures of metallic silicates. Glass is, however, amorphous; that is, it is not crystalline in structure. If silica is the necessary constituent of these masking materials, it is clear that it has to be in a fairly large crystalline form. In fact, we seem to be back to the much discussed 'silicon chip'. It would also appear that low grade, i.e. much crazed, quartz crystals are just as effective as the semi-precious amethyst, and they are, of course, much easier to obtain. There is a ready supply of such crystals in the faults of the Lewisian Gneiss in the Shieldaig area, and in all subsequent experiments I used this source of material.

I was particularly interested to discover what quantity of this material was required to mask completely a stone of given weight; that is, I wanted to know how many quartz chips were needed to mask a standing stone. I decided that the best way of determining this was to set up two stones on the church gallery, screened at both ends so that if one stone were masked, there would be no line between them. Various quartz chips weighing from 0.26 to 10.75g were then placed on one of the stones, the weight of which was known, and the strength of the line between them was measured with the gyrometer. This procedure was then repeated with six other stones of different weight. It was not possible, unfortunately, to record the point of complete masking because there the reaction of the pendulum would be nil. The strength of the lines was, therefore, plotted against the weight of chips used and, as this proved to be a linear relationship, the line was extrapolated to determine the weight of chips needed to give 100 per cent masking for each of the seven stones.

As I have said above, I wanted to know the weight of chips required to give complete masking of a stone of given weight. I therefore divided the weight of chips required for each stone by the weight of that stone in kilos, thus obtaining the weight of

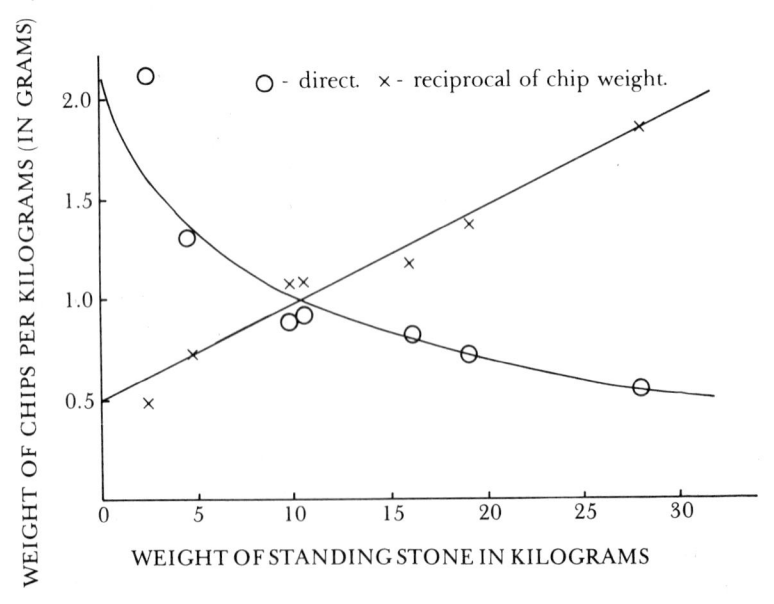

Figure 19. Weight of quartz chips per kilo of stone required to mask power of standing stone.

chips required per kilo of stone. These figures were then plotted against the weight of each stone (Figure 19, curve A). It appeared from this that the relationship was inverse; so I then replotted the graph, using this time the reciprocal of the weight of chips, and this gave a good straight line (Figure 19, curve B). Analysis of Covariance of these figures gave the best straight line that could be drawn through these seven points and a coefficient r = 0.9766.

I was still not satisfied that the best figures had been obtained from this investigation. I therefore plotted the reciprocal of the chips' weight against the power of the stones instead of against their weight. This seemed at the time to be a more reasonable hypothesis, since it was the power of the stones to form a line that one was trying to mask and one might have thought that the size of the charge might be important. However, on analysing these figures, I obtained a coefficient of r = 0.9206, which is probably not significantly worse than that for the weights, but is tending in that direction. I therefore concluded that the weight of chips required is more probably related to the weight of the stone concerned. From the analysis I obtained the equation:

$$1/y = 0.5045 + 0.04763 \, x \ldots \ldots 8(1)$$

where 'y' is the weight in grams of quartz chips per kilo of stone, and 'x' the weight of the stone in kilos.

It remained to try out this result in practice. As described above, the Rhu-na-Bidh Stone weighs 374 kilos, and from the above equation I found that 20.3g of chips should completely mask it. This stone has a number of lines running straight through it, but it also has one line coming from Meall Gharbhgair, which apparently ends here. If the stone were completely masked, this latter line should vanish, while the others would only be reduced in strength. I therefore found a quartz chip weighing about 21g and, having carefully located the exact whereabouts of this line with the Oasis Rod, I then placed the chip on the Rhu-na-Bidh Stone. I could then find no trace of the line from Meall Gharbhgair, and, on checking the remaining lines with the pendulum, I found that they were now much reduced in strength, since they were now travelling more than twice the distance from one stone to the next.

This masking effect of quartz crystals is apparently similar to Lethbridge's interrupters and seems to work if placed anywhere within the field round the charged object. From equation 8(1) it is clear that this interrupter needs to be present in sufficent quantities to have a full masking effect. Whether this is true of other interrupters is not known, but it is at least clear that much more work is needed to elucidate the mysterious properties of these materials.

This masking effect suggests a number of interesting explanations. As mentioned earlier, my church is built of dressed sandstone blocks on the outside and rough stone within, the intervening space being filled in with miscellaneous rubble. This rubble was undoubtedly collected locally from the surface of the Lewisian Gneiss and must, therefore, contain a fair proportion of the quartz and jasper found in the dykes. Any charge collected by the sandstone blocks when they were being dressed would therefore tend to be masked by the quartz in the rubble. This idea is supported by the observation that the charge on the church was not completely masked, i.e. there was insufficient quartz in the rubble, as shown by the weak lines I found running to the Rhu-na-Bidh Stone. Also, the charge on the church was still detectable inside the building, and in fact this was of an order that one might expect from a charge on the external stones. What happens when a charge is masked with quartz chips? No charge is detectable outside the stone, but it must still be present within, because it emerges again when the chips are removed. I see no ready means of testing this hypothesis short of removing all the rubble from the inside of the church walls — which, to put it mildly, is hardly practicable!

Recently Aubrey Burl (*Antiquity*, 54, 191-199, 1980) has studied a certain recumbent stone circle in the foot-hills of the Grampians. Here he found a large prostrate block set between the two tallest monoliths of the circle. Of particular interest was that he noted scattered round the prostrate stone, white quartz chips. His interpretation of this was that megalithic man had somehow associated this white quartz with the moon, an hypothesis which would be most difficult to test experimentally.

What is clear, however, is that these quartz chips would have masked the charge in the prostrate stone, but would not, of course, interrupt the flow of energy between the two adjoining tall stones, though they might at least reduce its strength. Without knowing the precise purpose for which the prostrate stone was intended, it is difficult to suggest why the builders should have wished to mask it, but it seems fairly clear that they must have known what would have been the results of scattering round a quartz interrupter.

If charged stones are set out in a circle, it must be concluded from what we have already discovered that lines will run from each stone to every other stone on the circumference. This is obviously rather wasteful of the stored energy and two alternative means of overcoming this are available, both of which appear to have been used by the megalithic builders. One way was to set a charged stone in the centre and thus gather all the power to this one stone. The other way was to scatter quartz chips inside the circle, but not within the fields of the circumference stones, and thus direct all the power round the circumference. Both these conditions have been described by Aubrey Burl[1] from his excavations of existing circles.

To test this idea, I set out on the lawn a circle of nine charged stones — a very common number according to Burl — with a radius of 4 metres. Nine stones give a circle of rather interesting geometry (Figure 20). Firstly, it can be readily set out with the aid of a straight edge and pair of compasses — items much favoured by the early geometers. Secondly, no stone is exactly opposite another on the circumference and although some 36 lines are formed in all, none actually pass through the centre; in fact, there is a small circle some 1.35 metres in diameter within such a circle of 4 metres radius that is completely free of lines.

In the exact centre of the circle I set a single stone, the charge of which I had already discovered to be 138.4 petrons. I then measured the charge on this stone with the portable gyrometer and found that it was now 155.7, a quite significant increase. this had obviously been caused by the lines running directly from the circumference stones (dotted in Figure 20). The next step was to place a number of quartz chips on each of these radial lines. These were 1.5 metres from the central stone and

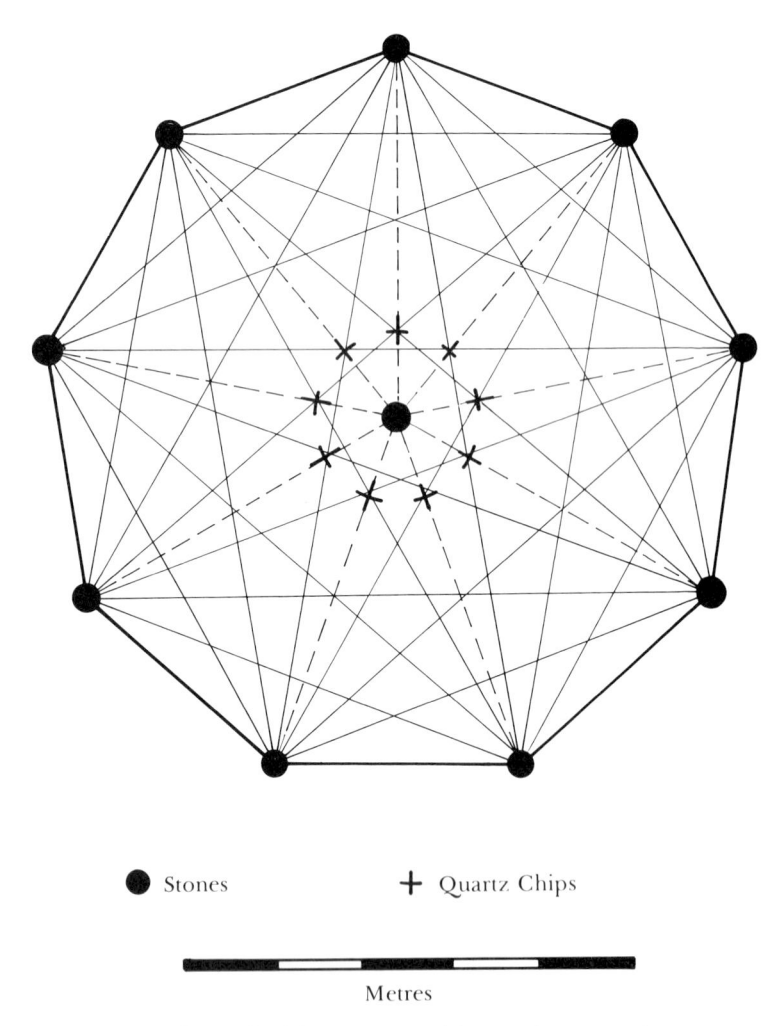

Figure 20. Effect of adding quartz chips and a central stone to a 9-stone circle.

therefore outside its field and also the line free circle mentioned above. I then again measured the charge on the central stone and found that it had now returned to the original value of 138.4. This would seem to prove that the quartz chips, at least under these conditions, were interrupting the lines running from the circumference to the central stone. Of course the remaining lines, as shown in Figure 20 would still be present and to interrupt these it would be necessary to scatter many more chips within the circle, but not within the fields of the surrounding stones that would then be masked. The only remaining lines would then be concentrated round the circumference.

In this experiment the quartz crystals appear to have been more effective in stopping the flow of the lines than was the case with the three stones in line, described above. With the circle, however, there was no stone opposite on the circumference when the central stone was blocked by the quartz.

Martin Brennan[1] mentions that the mounds in the Boyne Valley in Ireland were said to have been completely covered with white quartz chips. In his masterly decoding of the carvings on these stones, he has shown that these mounds were certainly designed for astronomical purposes — perhaps exclusively so. Since the stones on the mounds were heavily worked with carvings, they would certainly be charged and inevitably have entered the local ley complex. The megalithic builders would have been well aware of this and if they did not wish to disturb the ley environment by these structures, which were sited exclusively for astronomical purposes, they would have had to do something about it. Their answer was, of course, to give the mounds a complete capping of quartz chips, thus effectively masking their influence. There are rumours that these chips may be replaced and this will again remove their disrupting effect on the environment. Whether this has any calming effect on that troubled land remains to be seen.

Another example of the use of interrupters concerns the carved stone figures on Easter Island, which were so graphically described by Thor Heyerdahl in his book *Aku-aku.* He describes how these figures were cut out of the rocky hillside by hammering with stone hand-axes; they must, therefore, have received a strong charge from the field of the masons during this process. These figures were then set up in various parts of the island, thus causing a multitude of lines running from one to another. Now, the interesting point is that these figures were originally capped with a much smaller stone cylinder, the function of which was not apparent.

Heyerdahl puts forward the theory that these figures were carved and set up by a master race, possibly white, that had migrated from South America. In the course of time the indigenous population rebelled against their masters and destroyed many of these figures, in particular toppling the stone cylinders that had been placed on the figures' heads. Now, if the master race had been aware of the danger of an excess of lines covering the island, they could also have known that the charge they had given these figures during their construction could be nullified by capping with a suitable small stone. Records show that Easter Island was once much more fertile than is now the case and that it supported a large population. The natives would be ignorant of the significance of the stone caps and in destroying them they would have released all these lines, thereby causing a marked decrease in the fertility of the island — that is, of course, if my observations with the mustard seed are really significant. This again supports the disturbing speculation that perhaps we are even now in our ignorance destroying the fertility of the British Isles by fracturing the ancient ley lines with our modern civil engineering works.

In this book I have outlined full details for setting up a ley line. Should the reader be tempted to try this out himself, I would most strongly urge him not so to do. Two summers ago I was surprised to discover a number of small cairns of stones built on many of the hill tops around here, presumably by some holidaymaker. As I had not noticed these previously, I tested them with my pendulum and this showed that these cairns were not charged and therefore no lines ran between them. Had the builder known how to charge the stones, untold damage would have been done to the local ley complex. As yet we have very little knowledge of the potential power for good or evil of this energy, although there are indications that it can be great. Until such a time as we have this knowledge, it is very undesirable to add to or alter the existing system. All of the many stones which I have charged during this investigation have been stored in a fully screened container or masked with quartz chips. I hope therefore that I have in no way contaminated this ancient environment.

To many this landscape appears natural and little changed since the retreat of the last Ice Age. To the discerning eye, however, it is clear that everywhere there are signs of modification by megalithic man. Indeed, these remains are far more frequent and widespread than those of the vanished crofting communities whose 'larachs' are restricted to a few rapidly disintegrating walls of croft homesteads and shieling sites.

# 10.
# Conclusions

In the previous chapters I have tried to tell the story of this investigation and of the various mental steps I went through in an attempt to elucidate the laws controlling the formation and properties of ley lines. Some of these steps proved false, such as the relationship between the psi factor and the standard swing, and I had to retrace my steps and try another avenue of approach. Other problems, such as that of the charge on the church walls, and also the possibility of ley energy being electromagnetic in form, did not resolve themselves until much later in the investigation. Some subjects, such as the mode of action of interrupters and the interaction of a multiple array of standing stones, proved more than I could tackle at present with my limited time and resources.

What must be made perfectly clear is that I did not set out on these investigations to prove that ley lines exist. As a dowser, I already **knew** that they did; but, of course, such knowledge is purely subjective and not available to convince anyone else. However, when one considers all the measurements I have made and described in previous chapters, I feel it must be conceded that I have been measuring something. Either this 'something' must be real or, as some critics of dowsing maintain, I was merely recording measurements of my own subconscious mind.

If such an opinion is to be maintained, it must be admitted that my subconscious mind harbours a master mathematician.

## CONCLUSIONS

Nearly all the results I have described were obtained by measuring with the gyrometer, the readings of which are not immediately related to the final figures, and this would therefore prevent the wilful controlling of the pendulum to obtain a required result. Moreover, the final figures, more often than not, completely mystified me, and their meaning was far from clear until I had given them a great deal of careful thought. This would mean that my subconscious mind would have had to contain the whole complex phenomenon in all its detail and was just feeding bits of it to my conscious mind to see if I could understand it. Such an hypothesis seems to me to be patently absurd, and it must be a much simpler explanation to admit that ley lines really do exist and that it was some form of real energy I was measuring. Indeed, this is supported by the evidence of the effect of this energy on the Cruciferae seedlings, since this observation was not based on any dowsing measurements.

If we are willing to admit that ley lines exist, what evidence is there that they were man-made and not just a natural phenomenon? It is clear that these lines of energy flow between man-made objects, such as the features listed by Watkins in his pioneer work; but were these objects merely placed on sites that already held a natural charge? The argument seems to hinge on the presence of blind springs and crossed streams, which always appear to be present at ley centres, but not at crossing stones. Are these two phenomena created by the standing stones, etc., or were the stones placed in that position because these two phenomena already existed? I felt it needed one final experiment to resolve this problem.

Underwood suggested that blind springs were part of the geodetic line complex, i.e. they were formed at the terminus of a line. I thought that I might be able to test this by breaking a line with a fine mesh wire-netting screen. I tried this first on the line running down the centre of the church, but found that the screen did not break the line. I then recalled that this line was not at floor level, being at the height of the eaves, and that I had already found that, to break a line, the screen had to be in the exact centre of the line concerned.

As mentioned previously, I had used the line running

between the Rhu-na-Bidh Stone and Meal Gharbhgair to test the effect of masking the stone. I therefore tried placing the wire-netting screen on this line and then testing with the Oasis Rod for any indication of the blind spring round the stone. I could find no sign of it; so it would appear that the blind spring was only present when the line terminated at the stone.

I have already suggested that a blind spring may be no more than an interference phenomenon at the terminus of a line. Underwood figures these blind springs as spirals. To test this I very carefully followed with the pendulum the lines of the blind spring at one end of the church's central line and found they appeared to be in the form of concentric circles. It is not easy to follow these lines, and either Underwood or I may be mistaken. If they are in the form of concentric circles, this would seem to support the idea that they are, indeed, interference figures, caused by the energy of the line flowing into the stone and then back again, rather than straight on through the Stone as with a continuous line.

However, in the article by A. V. Jones mentioned previously[11], he studied some blind springs around a standing stone and within earthworks. In each case he found an anticlockwise flowing spiral. This spiral was, however, distorted by the ramparts of the earthwork and tended to follow the sides of the banks. The interesting part is that when the area was later bulldozed flat, he found that the shape had reverted to an even spiral.

But what about the so called crossed streams, which also seem to be present at all standing stones? When I stopped the line with the wire-netting, as described above, I could find no sign of the crossed streams either, so perhaps they also are formed by the terminating line.

This experiment really only provides very subjective evidence, and one needs something rather more positive as proof; but it does seem rather far-fetched to maintain that by placing a wire-netting screen across an invisible line on the surface, one had banished from existence two underground streams. There is no evidence that substantiates the assertion that these crossed streams are, in fact, streams of water flowing below these sites. Possibly they are no more than lines of force below the ground surface that are influencing the dowser. This is supported by the contention that it is possible to check or divert 'black streams' by driving an iron stake into the surface. Even the most optimistic dowser would not claim, I think, that he had actually diverted, or stopped, a flow of water.

If all this is really true, it would appear that the exact locations at which megalithic man chose to place his ley centres were not ordained by some natural properties of the site but selected by him for whatever reasons that compelled him to set up this system. But what were the, presumably, cogent reasons for undertaking this vast amount of work? I am afraid that we still have only the vaguest ideas. What I have been able to show in the course of these investigations is that the energy of the lines and the energy stored in these stones, is inimical to certain forms of life; and if this energy is in any way related to that in black streams, this fact has been known to dowsers for a very long period of time. I do not think we are likely to be able to answer this question until we have a much deeper knowledge of what this energy really is.

During the course of these experiments I have discovered a number of properties of this energy that may give some leads as to its real nature. Firstly, it appears to form a field surrounding all living material, and in this it is not dissimilar to the electromagnetic fields found by Burr[5]. The fact that these charges can be transferred to stones and that their subsequent decay can be prevented by heat or an electromagnetic field, etc., would seem to support the idea that we are here dealing with some form of electromagnetic energy, as also does the fact that the strength of the line between two charged stones decreases as the stones are moved further apart. The rate of this decrease, however, is such that it appears we are dealing with a narrow beam of energy and not just an expanding field surrounding the stones. The further evidence that we can produce interference phenomena on these lines indicates that we are dealing with a wave formation and from this we can suggest that it has a wavelength of about one-half to two metres. If, therefore, this energy is electromagnetic in nature, it should not prove too difficult to design some form of electronic device that would detect and measure it with far more accuracy than I have been able to do with the aid of a pendulum and gyrometer. One is left, however, with a nasty feeling that if ley energy is electromagnetic in nature, it would surely by now have been detected by one of the immense range of electronic instruments already available to the modern physicist. What alternatives then have we to turn to?

A rather intriguing idea, recently put forward by Wing-Commander C. V. Beadon,[1] is that ley lines may be thought waves that pick up good or bad qualities as they travel through space. That such waves do exist is apparent from the effects they can have in such phenomena as psychokinesis and poltergeists. Unfortunately, this hypothesis would appear to be most difficult to test in the field, since, if we dismiss the materialistic contention that thought is nothing but the flow of electrical impulses from one brain cell to another, we are left with little conception as to what thought really is.

Beadon's idea is not, however, quite as revolutionary as it might at first appear. Recent ideas in theoretical physics[2] concerning the implications of the quantum theory and relativity, suggest that both matter and thought are merely explicate eruptions on an implicate sea of energy filling the whole of cosmic space. The properties of thought waves should, therefore, not be greatly different from those of the electromagnetic fields surrounding all matter. Further, Dom Petitpierre[18] has suggested that it may be possible to eradicate ley lines by a ceremony of exorcism; surely a purely mental exercise. This idea may also be a possible explanation of the rates found by Lethbridge for abstract concepts, which must exist only in pure thought.

Shortly before going to press, it was pointed out to me that as the human body has a charged field and also mass, according to my findings outlined in this book, one would expect that a line should form between two such bodies. This obviously had to be checked, so I decided to carry out one further experiment.

Two people (both female) were stationed 7.5 metres apart, in an area where I had found no lines to be present; both were given a stone to hammer in the left hand, so that I could determine their respective charges. They were then asked to direct their thoughts at each other's minds, and while they were doing this, I checked with the Oasis Rod that there was apparently a line running between them. I then placed a stone on this line, approximately halfway between them and hammered it. To ensure that I did not disturb this line with my own personal field, I used a hammer with a handle about a metre long.

The two participants were then asked to think of something else or, better still, keep their minds blank, and while they were doing this, I again checked with the Oasis Rod, but could now detect no line between them. To substantiate this, I hammered another unhandled stone on the position of the previous line.

The values of the charges on the stones they had held, together with the participants' weights, gave me a figure for their respective powers and from these I was able to calculate from Equation 6(3) (given in Appendix B) the theoretical strength of the line between them and found that this came to 97.3 petrons. However, on checking the charge on the stone hammered on the line when they had been directing their thoughts at each other, I obtained a figure of only 79.0 petrons. This difference is significant, but we have no reason to believe that the mass of the human body is equivalent to that of a quartz-containing stone, for which equation 6(3) was designed. It may well be that the body is much less efficient in the production of power. What is, however, very remarkable, is that I could detect with the Oasis Rod no line between them when their minds were directed elsewhere, nor could I detect a charge on the stone hammered at that time.

No doubt the sceptics will say that all this was only recorded by dowsing and that as it was presumably the result I expected I could easily have influenced the movement of my pendulum. To substantiate my findings, therefore, I grew a pot of seven mustard seeds on each of the two stones hammered on the line, using the technique described in Chapter 8. Germination was rather poor — the seed is now two years old — but the mean weight of the seedlings from the stone hammered when the two participants were directing their thoughts at each other was 73 mg while those from the stone when their minds were directed elsewhere or blank, proved to be 107 mg, thus showing a reduction by the line of 31.8 per cent.

This experiment obviously needs repeating by other

workers and with a lot more consideration given to guarding against the interference of external fields; for example the two participants should really be inside a wire-netting cage, with the experimenter outside, so that his field can have no influence on the experiment; moreover, he should be invisible so that the participants do not direct their attention — and a line — to him.

If, however, these findings can be substantiated, they are obviously of enormous significance. Not only do they tend to support Beadon's idea,[2] mentioned above, that ley lines may be thought lines, but also the idea put forward by many writers that these lines may have been used for communication purposes or may even be of importance in facilitating telepathy. What is interesting is that the line only appeared when the two human minds were directed at each other. Had they reacted in the same way as an inanimate stone, lines would have radiated out to all other charged bodies in the immediate vicinity. This observation would imply that in a crowded room one is not inflicted with lines from everyone around, but only from those with whom one is in immediate communication. This may help to explain the well-known 'cocktail party phenomenon', where one only hears the conversation of one's immediate neighbour in spite of the general buzz all round.

If the findings of this experiment are confirmed, it opens up a whole new conception of the ley line problem and one that is likely to prove very difficult to crack. All that we have discovered in this investigation points to the idea that this energy is biological in origin and that the ley complex was originally set up by megalithic man according to his own plan, rather than siting it on an already existing pattern of geodetic lines.

## Appendix A
# Measuring the Charge

I had noticed that the longer the cord (rate) of the pendulum, the larger the radius of gyration appeared to be. I made the assumption that the 'inherent' rates for each material, as described by Lethbridge, should remain constant, as opposed to the 'induced' rate such as I had found in the sling stones. I therefore selected some thirty different materials, each of which had a specific rate given by Lethbridge. Fifteen of these materials were minerals, such as silica, calcium, etc., or metals such as iron, copper, etc., while the remaining fifteen were organic substances such as certain plants, woods, etc. The rates of these materials covered practically the whole range from 0 to 100cm. I then measured the radius of gyration for each material, taking in all a little over a period of half-an-hour so that there would be no appreciable variation with time. These radii of gyration were then plotted against their respective rates, and I obtained a good straight line relationship, giving a ratio (S/R) of 0.2828 when the radius was divided by the rate. This process was repeated on another day, and I again obtained a good straight line relationship, but this time with a value of 0.1583 for the ratio.

This was a distinct complication, since it would mean that either the charges of the inherent rates were varying from day to day or my powers as a dowser controlling the pendulum were varying. If the former was the case, it meant that all the charges were varying in exactly the same way; so it seemed much more likely that it was I who was at fault. I therefore decided to see if I could detect any such variation in my powers as a dowser, and if such was the case, whether there was any detectable pattern in it.

In one of his books on dowsing[15c] Lethbridge describes a rate (22.5cm or 9½ inches) that he used to estimate the psychic potential of an individual, by counting the number of revolutions of the pendulum of this length before it returned again to oscillations. I had already tried this on myself, by holding the pendulum over my right toes and had noted that I seldom got the same figures twice. I therefore decided to see if this measurement had any relationship to the variations in the radius of gyration, which I had found on

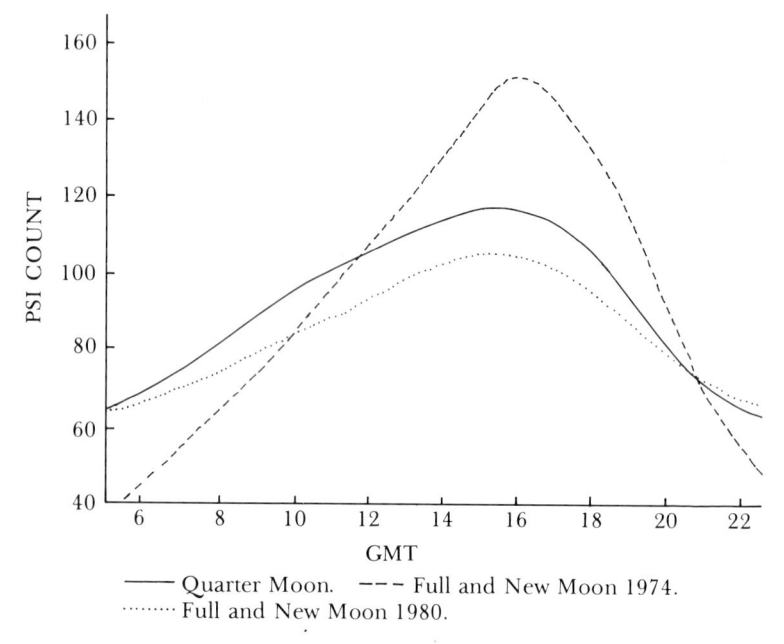

―― Quarter Moon.   ――― Full and New Moon 1974.
········· Full and New Moon 1980.

Figure 21. Circadian variations in psi count.

the inherent rates of these materials. One day, therefore, I made one of these 'psi' counts over my toes every hour from 6 a.m. to midnight and, on plotting the resulting figures against time, I obtained a smooth curve (Figure 21a): low at first and rising to a peak at about 4 p.m. (GMT), then falling again. I later managed to obtain a few other counts during the period between midnight and 6 a.m., which suggested that the minimum was at about 3 a.m., thus completing the curve. I repeated this exercise on another day, when I again obtained a smooth curve, but this time with much less difference between the peak and the trough. This meant that there was a marked circadian rhythm in my psi count, but that there was also some other factor that affected it from day to day.

As a biologist I was well aware that there are many biological rhythms related to the phases of the moon; so I decided to see if this was in any way concerned with the variations in my psi counts. Since the maximum of my circadian rhythm was at 4 p.m., I made a psi count over my toes at this hour every day for 29 days, thus covering all phases of the moon. On plotting these figures I again got a smooth curve with maxima at the full and change phases and minima at the first and third quarters. Combining these figures with those of the circadian rhythm, I obtained a series of seven curves, one for each day of the lunar month, with the maximum difference between

# APPENDIX A – MEASURING THE CHARGE

peak and trough in the curve for the full and change, and the minimum difference in the curve for the quarter moons.

All this had taken a long time to work out, about three months in fact, and several hundred counts, but I now had a good psi count for every hour of every day, over all phases of the moon. I now had to see if these psi counts were in any way related to the variations in the radius of gyration which I had previously encountered. To do this I used only two materials: zinc, which has the same inherent rate as male (60cm or 24 inches), and gold, which has the same rate as female (72.5cm or 28 inches). I had already collected quite a number of measurements of the radius of gyration (S) for these materials, together with the time of day and phase of the moon when they were made. I therefore plotted the ratio (S/R) of the radius of gyration to the rate (since I had already determined that this was constant at any one time for all materials) against my psi count for the time at which the measurement was made. These figures were subjected to an Analysis of Covariance, and I was relieved to find that I here had a highly significant ($P = 0.01$) relationship:

$$S_s = R(a + b\psi) \ldots \ldots A(1)$$

where $S_s$ is what I now called the standard swing, R the rate of the material and $\psi$ the psi count at the time the observation was made (a and b are constants). Thus, since $\psi$ was now known, it was possible to calculate from this formula the standard swing of any material with a rate of R. The values for a and b are constant for me, but may very well differ with other dowsers.

My next task was to see if this worked with materials in which the charge was induced rather than inherent. For this I selected six specimens: two grave stones with a male rate as described in Chapter 1, one being strong and the other weak; two with female rates; a flint arrowhead with a strong male rate; and an old pottery shard with a strong female reaction. The radius of gyration of each of these specimens was measured six times, with the time of day and phase of the moon carefully noted, so that a psi count could be assigned for each measurement. The full results were then subjected to an Analysis of Variance, giving a standard error of ± 2.056 about the overall mean of 106 for the six measurements I had made. Generally during later work I did three measurements of each specimen, two in the morning and one in the afternoon, so that that psi counts would be well spread out. Taking a mean of the three measured values obtained, I could generally rely on an error of about ± 3.18 per cent. This would not always be the case, however; the method of estimating the radius of gyration described above was to the nearest half centimetre on the scale of the gyrometer. A quarter centimetre when the radius was no more than 2 or 3 centimetres was obviously more important than an error of the same size when the radius was over 20 centimetres.

Errors are usually distributed round a mean in what is known as the normal curve, which is bell-shaped, with the peak at the mean value. An error distribution where it is largest at low values of the mean and decreases with an increase of mean is known as a Poisson Distribution. This does not mean, as one of my students remarked, that the whole set-up is extremely fishy, but was, I believe, named after the mathematician who first described it. He was able to show that an error of this type was proportional to the square-root of the mean.

With experience I found that I was dealing with values of charge varying from about 20 to 160. Since the determined error, as found from the Analysis of Variance, was ± 2.056 for a mean of six counts, we can calculate that for a mean of three counts of 20, the error would be ± 6.698 and, for one of 160, would be ± 2.367. This means that in dealing with comparison between two means near the lower values of charge, one would have to be very circumspect. However, most observations where, with values around 100 and with a standard error of about ± 2.9, I could be fairly certain that two means, separated by as little as 9, were in fact different with a probability of 1 in 20.

The charge in the specimen, be it male or female, I decided to express as a ratio, i.e. the observed radius of gyration $(S_o)$ divided by the standard swing $(S_s)$. Since the standard swing can be calculated from equation A(1) as shown above, $S_s$ can be substituted by $R(a + b\psi)$. So as to obtain values of a more reasonable size, I decided to multiply this ratio by 100. The charge (C) can therefore be calculated from the equation:

$$C = 100 S_o \div R(a + b\psi) \quad \ldots \ldots A(2)$$

Following the tradition of the physical sciences, I had to give this unit of charge some suitable name. Although many of the properties I had found in the investigations were in some ways similar to those of electricity, there were many differences, and I was anxious that no false conclusions should be drawn by using similar terms. Since I had called the lines that I had found running through my church petrostats, I decided to call this unit of charge a petron and to define the standard swing as 100 petrons. Thus, for example, if the observed swing was 1½ times the size of the standard swing, the charge of the specimen would work out at 150 petrons.

There is one particular danger in using an Analysis of Covariance, and that is of assuming that because there is a significant correlation between factors A and B, variations in A are the cause of the variations in B. A good example of this was given by Nigel Balchin in his novel *The Small Back Room*. He describes a rather bored boffin with a calculating machine finding a correlation between the figures for the penetration of bullets on a firing range and the heights of the soldiers firing. Realizing that their heights could not have any direct effect on the penetration, he speculates as to the real cause — such as that the air was more rarified at the level of the taller soldiers, or, if they were lying down, that they were nearer the target: both equally unlikely causes of the differences. He had in fact realized that, although the two factors were certainly related, there must be a third factor, not shown in the data, to which both were related. The discovery of a significant correlation must be examined with considerable circumspection before cause and effect are concluded as proved.

In trying to explain the results in my paper in the *Journal* of the British Society of Dowsers[11], I fell into this fundamental trap. I had examined these two rhythms in my personal psi counts and tried to find possible causes.

## APPENDIX A – MEASURING THE CHARGE

Taking the circalunar rhythm first, I was able to show that the differences in the radius of gyration found were probably due to the small effects of gravitation of the sun and moon together acting with, or against, that of the earth, over which the pendulum was swinging. The circadian rhythm was more difficult to explain, and I therefore assigned it to some biological changes affecting my psychic potential.

From equation A(1) given above, it is apparent that the $\psi$ I had been measuring was no more than the ratio of the observed swing to the standard swing for an inherent rate. Had I been measuring my psychic potential as a gyration of the pendulum at a rate of 22.5cm, it might have varied in the same way as for any other inherent factor and would not have suggested that my potential was varying. The important fact is that I had been measuring my psi count as the number of gyrations before the pendulum returned to oscillations. On the other hand, when examining the relationship between my psi count and the charge of stone held in the hand, as has been shown (Figure 8), I found that my personal field was in fact varying in the same manner. It seems clear, therefore, that the variations in my personal psi count were not the direct cause of the variations in the ratio S/R for inherent rates; but both must be related to some other factor having these circadian and circalunar rhythms. What was varying was some physical factor that affected both the radius of gyration and in the same way the number of gyrations of the pendulum before it returned to oscillations in the psi count. I had shown that one of these factors was possibly due to gravity, but the circadian rhythm remained a mystery.

Since publishing these results, a correspondent has suggested that perhaps these circadian rhythms are due to astrological influences. I am not sufficiently knowledgeable about this 'science' to be able to pass judgement on this; but, since the lunar rhythm was apparently due to gravitational effects, it does seem possible that this other rhythm was also due to some 'cosmic' influences. However, on examining the figures for these two rhythms, it appears that the amplitude of the circadian rhythm was nearly three times that of the circalunar, and it must be concluded, therefore, that, whatever factor was causing the circadian rhythm, it must have been much stronger than the gravitational effects of sun and moon.

It has been pointed out to me that, instead of getting involved with the complication of my psi counts, I could much more easily have measured the fluctuating relationship between the observed swing and the standard swing and plotted this against time. I have in fact subsequently employed this method for determining variations in the value of $\psi$, using the two metals zinc and gold. The above situation is often one of the difficulties in scientific research; we are faced with a complicated set of observations and look for some kind of hunch in an attempt to explain them. My first hunch was that the moon was having some sort of effect, and that Lethbridge's psi count might be a measure of this. I was lucky in that it turned out that the variations in my psi count were directly related to whatever was causing the variations in the size of the standard swing.

One curious fact has recently emerged. When I wrote the report on this technique[11], I stated that the psi counts had not varied from the time when they were first made in 1975 and the date of reporting in 1977. However, when in 1979 I was carrying out the observations on stones and lines described in the text, I noted that the standard swing I was getting in the afternoon counts was smaller than those in the morning, indicating that I was using a psi count for the afternoon that was too large. I therefore checked on the circadian rhythm, this time using the radius of gyration observed on samples of zinc and gold, and found that, indeed, the circadian curve for the first and third quarters of the moon had remained quite constant, but that the afternoon peak at the full and new moon had decreased from a figure of 152 to 128. This again happened when I checked the values for $\psi$ in the latter part of 1980, when the peak figure worked out at 107 (Figure 21). Thus the peak at full and new moon was now lower than at the quarter moons. This would seem to upset my theory that the circalunar rhythm was due to the interacting gravitational forces of the sun, moon, and earth, which surely could not have changed over this period. It would seem that the value of $\psi$ must be subject to a third rhythm, changing over a much longer period of time; how long remains to be seen. From the practical point of view it would appear essential that the values of $\psi$ must be checked at least every six months, if constant values for $S_x$ are to be maintained.

# Appendix B
# Loss in Strength of Line on Separating Two Charged Stones

As explained in the text (p.73) from these experiments I had only twelve results — including that from zero separation. I plotted these as a graph (Figure 22) relating the percentage loss in strength per metre of separation, against the joint power of the two stones at either end of the line. It is quite clear from this graph that the greater the joint power of these stones the less is the percentage loss in strength. Is this a direct relationship or something different? To test this I calculated an Analysis of Covariance for the following equation:-
$$y = a - bx$$
where y is the percentage loss of strength per metre of separation and x the joint power of the two stones. The results of this analysis are plotted as the straight line in Figure 22.

Let us examine the implications of this straight line. It would seem to indicate that when the joint power of the two stones is zero there would be a percentage loss per metre of 3.4 and that at a percentage loss of zero, the joint power would only be 15.9 lithons. On the face of it, both these predictions seem pretty unlikely. I therefore tried altering the equation to:
$$y = \frac{1}{c + dx}$$
and tried another Analysis of Convariance, which then gave me the curved line shown in the graph Figure 22. This suggests that at zero power the loss per metre is infinite, while at 1 lithon the loss would be 3.35 per cent. At 1000 lithons the predicted loss is only 0.00577 per cent per metre and it never actually falls to zero however large the power. This, therefore, seems to be the more reasonable solution. The analyses also showed that the second equation, giving the curved line, was a slightly better fit to the points and that this relationship was in fact highly significant (P = 0.01). I was then able to produce the formula:

134     LEY LINES – THEIR NATURE AND PROPERTIES

$$S_L = C_0 - \left(\frac{C_0 \times D}{24.4 + 5.45 \, \Sigma P}\right) \quad \ldots \ldots 6(3)$$

In this, $S_L$ is the strength of the line between the two stones, which is what we are trying to determine. The stones have a joint power of $\Sigma P$ expressed in lithons, and are separated by a distance of D metres. We first have to calculate the combined charge of the two stones when at zero separation ($C_0$) by using equation 6(1) and from this subtract the factor within the brackets. It will be seen that this factor is increased as D increases, but decreases as $\Sigma P$ grows larger. The two constants (24.4 and 5.45) are those derived from the analysis of the curved line in Figure 22.

This equation is called 6(3) throughout the text and was subsequently used to calculate the strength of a line between two stones when their weight and charge were known, together with the distance separating them. It must be made clear that this equation only holds good for two stones in isolation from all other influences. As is shown in the text, if there are other charged stones in the vicinity, a far more complex situation arises, which is not covered by this equation.

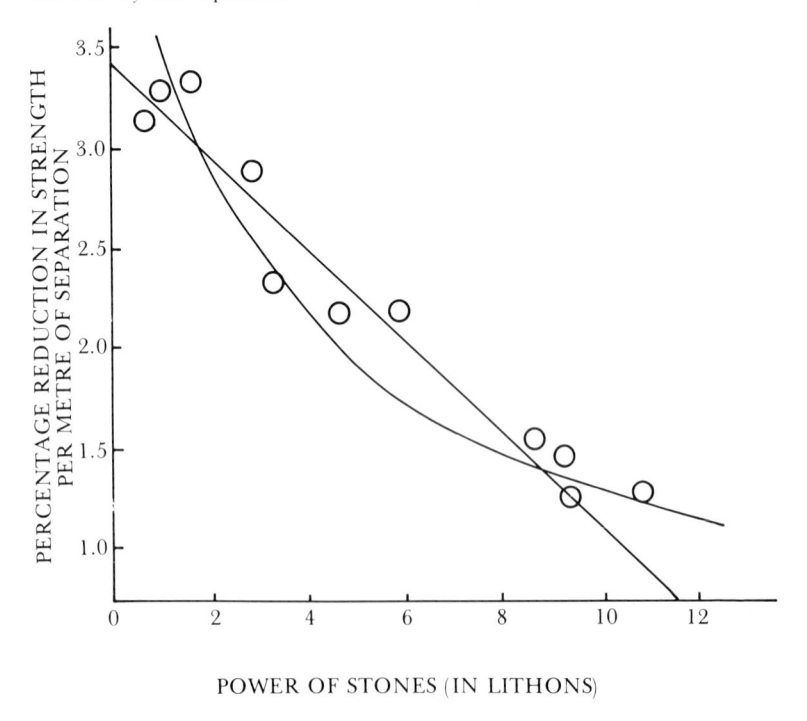

Figure 22. Effect of increasing stone power on percentage reduction in strength of line per metre of separation.

# Glossary

AQUASTAT This is one of the three types of geodetic line described by Underwood, and on which he claimed ancient buildings were sited. Aquastats appear to differ from the straight lines found in buildings by the present writer and termed petrostats (q.v.) in that they consist of two sets of triads with no central line and do not run straight. In spite of their name, aquastats do not appear to be connected with water.

BLACK STREAM A term used by water diviners to denote an underground stream that is not considered to be potable and that reacts to black on the Mager Circle. Some dowsers think that such 'streams' give off rays that are bad for the health of anyone living within their range.

BLIND SPRINGS Described by Underwood as forming the centres of primary spirals to which primary geodetic lines converge. Many dowsers have confirmed that ley centres (q.v.) are centred over blind springs. It is not certain that blind springs have, in fact, anything to do with water.

CHARGE This is the property of an object that causes the pendulum of a dowser to gyrate. A charge may be inherent or induced, and its size is measured with a gyrometer in petrons.

CIRCADIAN A term introduced by Franz Halberg *et al* (in *Photoperiodism and Related Phenomena in Plants and Animals,* Washington, 1959) to denote a rhythm with a natural period of about twenty-four hours. A circalunar rhythm has a natural period of about 29.5 solar days.

CROSSING STONES A term used by the present writer to designate a stone that marks the spot where two ley lines cross. A crossing stone differs from a ley centre in that it is not situated over a blind spring.

DECAY RATE The process in which the charge is lost from an object when it has been moved from a charged field. It is shown that the decay rate is constant whatever the charge and that it is exponential in form, with a half-life of about three hours.

FIELD An area surrounding a charged object, in which the pendulum reacts to the charge. T. C. Lethbridge noted that this field was in the form of a circle of a radius equal to the rate of the field. This circle, he stated, formed the base of cones extending both above and below the object.

FIXING A process, described by the writer, by which the charge is permanently fixed into an object placed within the field of another charged object. Without this process of fixing, the charge taken up by that object gradually decreases (decays) when removed from the charged field, and is ultimately lost.

GYROMETER An instrument designed by the author for measuring the radius of gyration of a pendulum held by the dowser over a charged object. This records what is termed the 'observed swing' (q.v.) at the time.

INDUCED CHARGE When an object, e.g. a stone, is placed within the field of another charged object, it takes up that charge, which is then said to be induced. This will ultimately decay away when it is removed from the field unless it is then 'fixed'. The induced charge is measured in petrons.

INHERENT CHARGE T. C. Lethbridge showed that all objects, and even abstract ideas such as courage and country of origin etc., have an inherent charge which is related to the length of the pendulum cord (rate) used to measure it. The present writer has been able to show that if the 'radius of gyration' (q.v.) of an inherent charge, i.e. the 'standard swing' is divided by the appropriate rate, a constant is obtained at any one time, but this varies as the 'psi factor' (q.v.) varies with time.

INTERRUPTERS A term introduced by Lethbridge to cover the properties of certain materials which, when placed within the field of another substance, interrupt the specific gyrations of the pendulum. He noted that they can have a variety of properties, having their own rate and perhaps a sex rate, but interrupt that of another. An interrupter may reverse a sex rate or neutralize another interrupter. There are many variations in this property.

LEY LINES Defined by Devereux and Thomson[6] as 'alignments of sites which ley hunters believe were surveyed and marked in pre-history'. The generally accepted criteria is five such sites in 25 miles. Others, particularly dowsers, define a ley in terms of straight lines of energy between sites, rather than their alignment, and this is the definition used in the present work.

LEY CENTRE Here defined as a charged point that always lies over a blind spring and crossed streams, and from which radiate ley lines — usually seven in number.

LITHON (From the Greek *lithos*, a stone). A unit of the power of a charged stone, and the product of the charge measured in petrons, multiplied by the mass in terms of kilograms. Thus, a stone weighing 1 kilo and with a charge of 100 petrons, is said to have a power of 1 lithon.

LONG PENDULUM The type of dowsing pendulum described by Lethbridge. It has a cord 40 inches long and each concept has its own length of cord, when the pendulum will then gyrate. The present writer uses a pendulum cord 1 metre in length, and the rates (q.v.) are measured in centimetres from the centre of gravity of the plumb bob to the point at which the cord is held. The cord is marked every 10cm with a coloured bead to facilitate measurement.

MAGER CIRCLE A disc divided into eight coloured segments, commonly used by water diviners to test the potability of underground water. The colours of the segments, going clockwise, are black, white, purple, blue, green, yellow, red, and grey. The actual colour assigned to a property varies somewhat between dowsers. Other things than water can also react to the Mager colours: thus a positive (male) ley line reacts to blue and a negative (female) one to white. Each colour also has its own Lethbridge rate.

MASKING A term used in this work to denote the effect of an interrupter (q.v.) on a charged stone etc. It does not remove the charge, but if present in sufficient quantity, the interrupter effectively prevents the charge having any external influence. On removal of the interrupter, the charge reappears, proving that it had only been masked.

PARALLEL A term used by Underwood to describe the parallel lines that run on either side of the centre of a geodetic line, at a distance equal to the rate. They would appear to be made up of the outer circumferences of the line of circular fields surrounding the central line. There is some evidence that there is a further pair of parallels about four metres on either side of a ley line.

PETROSTAT A term invented by the writer to designate a straight, charged line running through a stone building. In view of the fact that it seems to have the same properties as a ley line, it can probably be considered as equivalent, although it obviously does not fit the generally accepted definition of a ley line.

## 138   LEY LINES – THEIR NATURE AND PROPERTIES

OBSERVED SWING The radius of gyration (q.v.) of the pendulum when held over a charged specimen. This radius is measured by means of a gyrometer. It varies according to the rate, time of observation, and charge of the specimen.

PETRON (From the Greek *petros*, a rock). A unit of charge of a stone or other object. It is defined as the ratio between the standard swing for a particular rate, and the observed swing, the former being taken as 100. Thus, if the standard swing is calculated as a radius of gyration of 10cm at the time of observation, and the observed swing is found to be 15cm, the specimen in question is said to have a charge of 150 petrons.

POLARITY Dowsers maintain that charge, power, and strength can be either positive (rate 60cm) or negative (rate 72.5cm). These are said to be equivalent to male/female and to Yang/Yin. Lines also appear to indicate a colour on the Mager Circle, the male/positive lines being blue, and the female/negative lines being white. This is said to relate to the Blue Dragon and White Tiger of ancient Chinese Geomancy, as described by Eitel.[7]

POWER The property of a charged stone that enables it to radiate ley lines, being the product of the charge multiplied by the mass (weight). The degree of power is measured in lithons.

PSI FACTOR (From the Greek letter $\psi$ psi). A term invented by Lethbridge as a measure of the psychic potential of a dowser. It is measured by the number of gyrations of a pendulum with a cord 22.5cm long, before it again returns to oscillations. The present writer found that the value of the psi factor varied with the phases of the moon and also had a circadian rhythm.

RADIUS OF GYRATION The radius of a circle round which a pendulum gyrates when held by a dowser over a charged specimen. It varies in size with the rate and also with the psi factor. It is measured in centimetres with a gyrometer.

RATE A term invented by Lethbridge to indicate the length of the cord of a dowser's pendulum. Everything has its own specific rate, although, of course, some rates are common to several objects or ideas. In this book the rate is measured in centimetres from the centre of gravity of the bob to the point on the cord at which it is held by the dowser.

SHORT PENDULUM The pendulum used by the majority of dowsers. It usually has a cord of about 15-20 centimetres long, and it is used to reply to specific mental questions posed by the dowser, either by oscillating or gyrating clockwise or anticlockwise. The interpretation of the response varies with individual dowsers. The form of the

# GLOSSARY

question posed has to be chosen with great care, or an ambiguous reply may be returned.

STANDARD SWING The radius of gyration when measuring the inherent charge of a specimen. For any given rate, the standard swing can be calculated from the psi factor at the time of the observation.

STRENGTH A measure of energy in a line, be it a ley line, petrostat, aquastat, etc. It can be measured by observing the radius of gyration with a gyrometer and can thus be defined in terms of petrons.

TRIAD A term introduced by Underwood to denote the form of geodetic lines. Thus, each main line is made up of three minor lines, which together form a triad.

WATER LINE A particular type of geodetic line described by Underwood and thought by him to indicate a flow of underground water. Except that water lines do not run in straight lines, or above ground, they have similar dowsing characteristics to ley lines, i.e. a central triad with parallel triads at some distance on either side.

# References

1. Beadon, C. V., 'Ley Lines and Black Streams — Fact or Fancies?', *Journal of the British Society of Dowsers*, XXVII, 242 (1980).
2. Bohm, David, *Wholeness and the Implicate Order,* Routledge and Kegan Paul (1980).
3. Brennan, Martin, *The Boyne Valley Vision,* The Dolman Press (1980).
4. Burl, Aubrey, *Circles of Stone,* Weidenfeld and Nicolson (1979).
5. Burr, H. S., *Blueprint for Immortality,* Neville Spearman (1971).
6. Devereux, P. and Thomson, Ian, *The Ley Hunter's Companion,* Thames and Hudson (1979).
7. Eitel, E. J., *Feng Shui,* Pentacle Books (1979).
8. Fidler, J. H., 'Dating with the Pendulum', *Journal of the British Society of Dowsers*, XXIV, 45 (1974).
9. Fidler, J. H., 'With a Pendulum amongst the Larachs', *Journal of the British Society of Dowsers*, XXV, 178 (1976).
10. Fidler, J. H., 'Multidimensional Leys', *The Ley Hunter,* 83 (1978).
11. Fidler, J. H., 'A Technique for the Measurement of the Energy of Ley Lines by Dowsing', *Journal of the British Society of Dowsers*, XXVII, 175 (1980).
12. Graves, Tom, *Needles of Stone,* Turnstone Books (1978).
13. Jenkins, Stephen, *Undiscovered Country,* Neville Spearman (1977).
14. Jones, A. V., 'Accident or Design?', *Journal of the British Society of Dowsers*, XXVIII, 194 (1981).

15 Lethbridge, T. C.,
   (a) *ESP Beyond Time and Distance,* RKP (1965).
   (b) *A Step in the Dark,* RKP (1967).
   (c) *The Monkey's Tail,* RKP (1969).
   (d) *The Legend of the Sons of God,* RKP (1972).
   (e) *The Power of the Pendulum,* RKP (1976).

16 Lonegren, Sig, 'Notes from New England', *The Ley Hunter,* 91 (1981).

17 Michell, John, *City of Revelation,* Garnstone Press (1973).

18 Petitpierre, Dom Robert, *Exorcising Devils,* Robert Hale (1976).

19 Reichenbach, Carl von, *The Mysterious Odic Force,* Aquarian Press (1977).

20 Robins, Don, 'The Dragon Stirs', *Alpha,* 3, 16 (1979).

21 Screeton, Paul, *Quicksilver Heritage,* Thorsons (1974).

22 Smith, Sister Dr Justa, 'Significant Results in Enzyme Activity from Healer's Hands', Newsletter of the Parapsychology Foundation (January-February 1969).

23 Thom, A. and Thom, A. S., *Megalithic Remains in Britain and Brittany,* Oxford (1980).

24 Watkins, Alfred, *The Old Straight Track,* Methuen (1925).

25 Watkins, Alfred, *The Ley Hunter's Manual,* Simpkin Marshall (1927), reprinted, with an introduction by John Michell, Turnstone Press (1983).

26 Underwood, Guy, *The Pattern of the Past,* Museum Press (1969).

# Index

Applecross, 20, 33, 37-8
Aquastats, 24, 31, 135

Beadon, C.V., 124, 126
Beltane, Feast of, 34, 57, 102
Black streams, 135
Blind springs, 25, 39, 58, 92, 121, 122, 135
Bohm, David, 124
Brennan, Martin, 117
Burl, Aubrey, 56, 114
Burr, H.S., 123

Callanish, 38
Camus Beithe Stone, 35, 37, 79
Carnac, 61
Charge, 48, 130, 135
Circadian rhythm, 128, 135

Decay rate, 55, 136
Devereux, Paul, 136
Doire-aona, 93
Dowsers, British Society of, 31, 46, 47, 130
Dragon Project, 43

Dunne, J.W., 63

Easter Island, 117-118
Eitel, E.J., 107, 138

Fisher, R.A., 44

Graves, Tom, 40, 58, 89
Gyrometer, 46, 136

Heyerdahl, Thor, 117

Interrupters, 65, 69, 109f, 136

Jenkins, Stephen, 36
Jones, A.V., 50, 122

*Ley Hunter, The*, 33, 43, 101
*Ley Hunter's Manual, The*, 33
Laser effect, 99-100
Lethbridge, T.C., 17, 29, 47, 50, 64, 107, 127
Lewisian Gneiss, 28, 60, 93, 111
Lithon, 67, 137

Lonegren, Sig, 101
Long pendulum, 18, 48, 137

Maelrubha, St, 20
Map dowsing, 49
Michell, John, 38
Mustard seedlings, 102-105

Oasis rod, 25, 33
Observed swing, 48, 129, 138
*Old Straight Track, The*, 32

Petitpierre, Dom Robert, 124
Petrons, 48, 130, 138
Petrostats, 31, 137
Power, 67, 138
Psi factor, 47, 63, 127, 138

Rates (Lethbridge's), 18, 46, 138
Reich, Wilhelm, 43
Reichenbach, Karl von, 97
Rhu-na-Bidh Stone, 34, 79, 92, 98, 113, 122

Robins, Dr Don, 43, 57

Screeton, Paul, 89, 101
Short pendulum, 17, 48, 138
Shieldaig Old Church, 17, 26-28, 92, 114
Smith, Sister Justa, 105
Standard swing, 46, 130, 139
Stonehenge, 61, 99
Strength, 68, 139

Thom, A. and A.S., 23, 61, 91, 99
Torridonian Sandstone, 28, 60, 93, 111
Track lines, 24

Water lines, 24, 139
Watkins, Alfred, 32, 40, 89, 102, 121
Wavelength (of ley lines), 97-98

Underwood, Guy, 24, 30, 39, 89, 92, 102, 121